MW00938536

Trust in the Lord with all thine heart; and lean not unto thine own understanding. (Proverbs 3:5 KJV)

Trust in the Lord with all thine heart; and lean not unto thine own understanding. (Proverbs 3:5 KJV)

Daily Devotions

with

Jen

God Loves You . . . Truth, Faith, Reflection

JENNIFER TAYLOR

Edited by Jennifer Skinnell

Trust in the Lord with all thine heart; and lean not unto thine own understanding. (Proverbs 3:5 KJV)

Copyright © Jennifer Taylor

All rights reserved. No part of this book may be used or reproduced by any means, graphic, electronic, or mechanical, including photocopying, recording, taping or by any information storage retrieval system without the written permission of the author except in the case of brief quotations embodied in critical articles and reviews.

This book is a work of non-fiction. Unless otherwise noted, the author makes no explicit guarantees as to the accuracy of the information contained in this book and in some cases, names of people and places have been altered to protect their privacy.

Scripture taken from the King James Version of the Bible.

Scripture quotations marked (NIV) are taken from the Holy Bible, New International Version®, NIV®, Copyright © 1973, 1978, 1984, 2011 by Biblica, Inc. ™ Used by permission of Zondervan. All rights reserved worldwide. www.zondervan.com. The "NIV" and "New International Version" are trademarks registered in the United States Patent and Trademark Office by Biblica, Inc.™

Scripture quotations are taken from the Holy Bible, New Living Translation, copyright ©1996, 2004, 2007, 2013, 2015 by Tyndale House Foundation. Used by permission of Tyndale house Publishers, Inc., Carol Stream, Illinois 60188. All rights reserved.

The Holy Bible, English Standard Version® (ESV®) Copyright © 2001 by Crossway, a publishing ministry of Good News Publishers. All rights reserved. ESV® Text Edition: 2016

Because of the dynamic nature of the Internet, any web addresses or links contained in this book may have changed since publication and may no longer be valid. The views expressed in this work are solely those of the author.

Cover photo by Tiffany Kristine Photography

Trust in the Lord with all thine heart; and lean not unto thine own understanding. (Proverbs 3:5 KJV)

Dedication

I dedicate this book to anyone who has struggled with renewing their faith. These devotions go out to the hopeless so that they may know that Jesus loves them, and through Him they will obtain the peace and love they seek.

Trust in the Lord with all thine heart; and lean not unto thine own understanding. (Proverbs 3:5 KJV)

Introduction

Devotions are defined as love, loyalty or enthusiasm for a person, activity, or group. With God's continuous love for us, it is necessary to devote our time and energy toward his teachings. *Daily Devotions with Jen* focuses on God's love and compassion for our world. Through prayer and daily reminders, we are able to refocus and create a more positive mindset. These reminders offer hope and a fresh renewal of our faith.

Create in me a clean heart, O God;
And renew a right spirit within me. (Psalm 51:10 KJV)

When you stop and think about how much of your time is spent on worry and doubt, is there any room left for peace and optimism? It is important to take time each day to rest and refocus your mind on God's purpose for your life. A helpful way to regain a positive outlook on your days is to read the Bible. Through scripture, we reconnect with God, his Son, and the Holy Spirit. Scripture transforms our hearts and minds by opening our souls to new beginnings.

Hast thou not known? Hast thou not heard, that the everlasting God, the Lord, the creator of the ends of the earth, fainteth not, neither is weary? There is no searching for his understanding. He giveth power to the faint; and to them that have no might he increaseth strength. Even the youths shall faint and be weary, and the young men shall utterly fall; But they that wait upon the Lord shall renew their strength; they shall mount up with wings as eagles; they shall run, and not be weary; and they shall walk, and not faint. (Isaiah 40:28-31 KJV)

Trust in the Lord with all thine heart; and lean not unto thine own understanding. (Proverbs 3:5 KJV)

Daily Devotions with Jen provides scripture along with positive, yet straight forward reminders that you are loved and never alone. God's plan for your life is clearly written in his teachings and best followed on a daily basis.

Trust in the Lord with all thine heart; and lean not unto thine own understanding. In all thy ways acknowledge him, and he shall direct thy paths. (Proverbs 3:5-6 KJV)

Trust in the Lord with all thine heart; and lean not unto thine own understanding. (Proverbs 3:5 KJV)

Preface

I have designed this book to be taken with you on your daily travels. The devotions in *Daily Devotions with Jen* are reminders of God's unfailing love for you. My devotions are designed to help you live your days full of hope and optimism. I have also included space for your own Personal Reflection. When in doubt, open *Daily Devotions with Jen* and take in God's Word. It will lift your spirits and leave you feeling full of gratitude!

Trust in the Lord with all thine heart; and lean not unto thine own understanding. (Proverbs 3:5 KJV)

♥ His Word Heals ♥

For at one time you were darkness, but now you are light in the Lord. Walk as children of light. (Ephesians 5:8 ESV)

After receiving His Word in my life, how could I ever turn away! It has healed me, educated me, guided me and has given me purpose. How has His Word changed you? Let us be thankful for His love every day. It gives us light in our dark moments and shelter from the storms we face. If you read the Bible and have trouble understanding its contents, I urge you to join a study group or maybe create one. It's worth sharing with everyone we know.

~Let the Light of His Word Heal You~

Personal Reflection . . .

_____
_____
_____
_____
_____
_____
_____
_____
_____
_____
_____
_____
_____

Trust in the Lord with all thine heart; and lean not unto thine own understanding. (Proverbs 3:5 KJV)

♥Did You Know♥

These six things doth the Lord hate: a proud look, a lying tongue, and hands that shed innocent blood, an heart that deviseth wicked imaginations, feet that be swift in running to mischief, a false witness that speaketh lies, and he that soweth discord among brethren. (Proverbs 6:16-19 KJV)

Are we not called to be brothers and sisters in Christ? Are we not called to love as our Father has loved us? Are we not called to help those in need? So why gossip? Why slander the names of those whom you do not know? Why lie? Why place judgment on others who disagree with you? Are you truly thinking before you speak? Before you act? Are political differences causing tension in your relationships? Parenting style differences? Work and personal relationship stress? Are you truly aware that your words matter? Are you aware that your negative actions are mimicked and only bring others pain? Are you aware that Christ lives in you? Are you aware that He wants the best for you? Did you know that He died so that we could live as brothers and sisters? In peace? In forgiveness? Did you know we are to take up our cross and follow Him? Did you know that gossip only makes you look foolish? Did you know you have the power to be kind? Did you know it turns people away when you are negative and wicked in your actions?

~Scripture Is Truth, not Always Sugarcoated to Appease Your Temporary Needs~

Trust in the Lord with all thine heart; and lean not unto thine own understanding. (Proverbs 3:5 KJV)

Personal Reflection . . .

_____

_____

_____

_____

_____

_____

_____

_____

_____

_____

_____

_____

_____

_____

_____

_____

_____

_____

_____

_____

_____

_____

_____

_____

_____

_____

_____

_____

_____

Trust in the Lord with all thine heart; and lean not unto thine own understanding. (Proverbs 3:5 KJV)

♥Words Have Never Been More Important♥

Pleasant words are as a honeycomb, sweet to the soul, and health to the bones. (Proverbs 16:24 KJV)

Kind words: love, like, beautiful, sweet, pure, truth, helpful, thank you, bless you, be careful, grateful, how are you, I appreciate you, I accept you, I believe in you, I'm proud of you, you're welcome, Jesus loves you, you are unique, I trust you, you're smart.

Unkind words: you're weird, you're ugly, you've gained weight, you're stupid, gross, hate, unfriendly, creepy, evil, cruel, God doesn't exist, you are a mistake, you're embarrassing, you're not good enough, or you're worthless.

See the difference? Parents to children and children to parents, be kind! Co-workers and bosses to one another, be kind! Politicians to one another, be kind! Teachers to students and students to teachers, be kind! Husbands to wives and wives to husbands, be kind! Neighbors be kind! There is so much love in our world, so be sure to share it. That is what we were called to do!

Personal Reflection . . .

_____
_____
_____
_____
_____
_____
_____

Trust in the Lord with all thine heart; and lean not unto thine own understanding. (Proverbs 3:5 KJV)

❤*Go and Stay*❤

Am I a God at hand, declares the Lord, and not a God far away? Can a man hide himself in secret places so that I cannot see him? Declares the Lord. Do I not fill heaven and earth? Declares the Lord. (Jeremiah 23:23-24 ESV)

God isn't some small trifle idea of a being. He is the most almighty, Holy, and sovereign being known to man! He is our safe place, our Father in times of need and in times of joy. There is nothing more reassuring than His everlasting love for us. He wants you; He wants your love, devotion, and praise. He absolutely deserves it just as much as you deserve peace in your life.

~In All Your Ways Recognize Him~

Personal Reflection . . .

_____

_____

_____

_____

_____

_____

_____

_____

_____

_____

_____

_____

_____

Trust in the Lord with all thine heart; and lean not unto thine own understanding. (Proverbs 3:5 KJV)

♥Take Responsibility♥

For each will have to bear his own load. (Galatians 6:5 ESV)

He who plants and he who waters are one, and each will receive his wages according to his labor. (1 Corinthians 3:8 ESV)

Working hard and having integrity go hand in hand. Working hard and complaining do not! Actions are self-inflicting habits that will determine a negative or positive outcome. Actions are deeds, maneuvers, efforts and acts. So, ask yourself this question—Are my actions helping or hurting myself and others? For Jesus did not die for us to behave out of anger and revenge. He died so that we can live in peace as brothers and sisters in His Holy name. It is NEVER too late to make things better. Take responsibility, take positive action and set a positive example.

~Let us not be Fooled, for God is Always Watching~

Personal Reflection . . .

_____
_____
_____
_____
_____
_____
_____
_____
_____
_____

Trust in the Lord with all thine heart; and lean not unto thine own understanding. (Proverbs 3:5 KJV)

♥Goodness and Beauty Shall Reign♥

How beautiful upon the mountains are the feet of him that bringeth good things, that publisheth peace; that bringeth good tidings of good...Thy God reigneth! (Isaiah 52:7 KJV)

Our God of Peace bestows beauty upon our world. His creation is His vision of the beauty that we are blessed to live in. Let us be responsible for taking care of it and one another. The wonders of new beginnings are around every corner and new in each season that is set before us. What you carry from yesterday leave in the wind, and step into today with new Faith. This new Faith will set your heart and soul free. This new Faith will allow you to believe that goodness and beauty shall reign forever.

~Blessed are They who Renew Their Faith~

Personal Reflection . . .

_____

_____

_____

_____

_____

_____

_____

_____

_____

_____

_____

Trust in the Lord with all thine heart; and lean not unto thine own understanding. (Proverbs 3:5 KJV)

♥Can You♥

My soul, wait thou only upon God. (Psalm 62:5 ESV)

When the cares of my heart are many, your consolations cheer my soul. (Psalm 94:19 ESV)

Now is the time to let God do everything you cannot. Now is the time to let go of what's weighing on your heart. Now is the time to go to Him. We truly do make life harder on ourselves than we need to. We complain and we allow our burdens take over our good judgment. Are you holding onto hate? Are you holding onto revenge? Or are you desperate to let these things go? If God wants your burdens, and He wants to heal your soul, let Him! Don't we want to heal our children when they are hurting inside? Of course, we do.

Casting all your anxieties on him, because he cares for you. (1 Peter 5:7 ESV)

Personal Reflection . . .

_____

_____

_____

_____

_____

_____

_____

_____

_____

_____

Trust in the Lord with all thine heart; and lean not unto thine own understanding. (Proverbs 3:5 KJV)

♥What's Going on That's Frightening You♥

Always remember Trust in the Lord with all your heart, and lean not on your own understanding. (Proverbs 3:5 KJV)

Have I not commanded you? Be strong and courageous. Do not be frightened, and do not be dismayed, for the Lord your God is with you wherever you go. (Joshua 1:9 ESV)

How many times a day do you tell our Lord that you trust Him? I do it every single day! I have to! There is nothing that keeps me more grounded than placing my hope, confidence, and full trust in His hands. This has allowed me to move past things I cannot control. I'm a worrying mom and wife on a daily basis. What I've learned, however, is that it's not healthy to live this way. It's not healthy for anyone! We are all missing out on joyful occasions when we become consumed with worry, anxiety and doubt. God has commanded us to trust Him, so let's do it. He IS in control, not you and not me. Talk to Him today and tell Him you trust in His ultimate plans.

The Lord is my strength and my shield; in Him my heart trusts, and I am helped; my heart exults, and with my song I give thanks to Him. (Psalm 28:7 ESV)

Personal Reflection . . .

_____

_____

_____

_____

_____

_____

Trust in the Lord with all thine heart; and lean not unto thine own understanding. (Proverbs 3:5 KJV)

❤Your Word Is Truth❤

Stand therefore, having fastened on the belt of truth, and having put on the breastplate of righteousness. (Ephesians 6:14 ESV)

The Bible is full of scripture, consisting of 66 books of the Old and New Testaments. It's not meant to sugarcoat how you live your life. It's meant to guide you down a path of righteousness. Its truths scare people with their ears closed off to them. Truth can be scary, especially when it goes against your own ideologies.

Sanctify them in truth; your word is truth. (John 17:17 ESV)

And you will know the truth, and the truth will set you free. (John 8:32 ESV)

Personal Reflection . . .

_____
_____
_____
_____
_____
_____
_____
_____
_____
_____
_____
_____
_____

Trust in the Lord with all thine heart; and lean not unto thine own understanding. (Proverbs 3:5 KJV)

♥ His Presence Offers Hope You've Never Experienced ♥

Through him we have also obtained access by faith into his grace in which we stand, and we rejoice in hope of the Glory of God. (Romans 5:2 ESV)

Now faith is the assurance of things hoped for, the conviction of things not seen (Hebrews 11:1 ESV)

I love speaking on the importance of having hope. When God says your faith can move mountains, it absolutely can! Hope takes us to the next level in life; it takes us closer to Him. When we place our trust, faith and hope in His hands, we truly can do anything. I held onto hope so tightly when I faced difficulties in my personal and professional life. Hope took me to the next phase, and then the next phase, and now I'm here trying to help those who struggle in their faith. Hope allows us to NOT quit. Keep your Hope alive. Keep your faith strong. You will never regret it!

Fear not, for I am with you; be not dismayed, for I am your God; I will strengthen you, I will help you, I will uphold you with my righteous right hand. (Isaiah 41:10 ESV)

Personal Reflection . . .

_____
_____
_____
_____
_____

Trust in the Lord with all thine heart; and lean not unto thine own understanding. (Proverbs 3:5 KJV)

❤ Beatitudes ❤

The Beatitudes mean blessedness, benediction, and grace. They are eight blessings (teachings) recounted by Jesus in the Sermon on the Mount, found in the Gospel of Matthew. I believe they speak for themselves.

And seeing the multitudes, he went up into a mountain: and he was set, his disciples came unto him: And he opened his mouth, and taught them, saying
Blessed are the poor in spirit: for theirs is the kingdom of heaven.
Blessed are they that mourn: for they shall be comforted.
Blessed are the meek: for they shall inherit the earth.
Blessed are they which do hunger and thirst after righteousness: for they shall be filled.
Blessed are the merciful: for they shall obtain mercy.
Blessed are the pure in heart: for they shall see God.
Blessed are the peacemakers: for they shall be called the children of God.
Blessed are they which are persecuted for righteousness' sake: for theirs is the kingdom of heaven.
(Matthew 5:1-10 KJV)

Personal Reflection . . .

_____
_____
_____
_____
_____
_____
_____

Trust in the Lord with all thine heart; and lean not unto thine own understanding. (Proverbs 3:5 KJV)

♥ Make Your Heartfelt Requests Known ♥

Continue in prayer, and watch in the same with thanksgiving.
(Colossians 4:2 KJV)

Dear Heavenly Father,

I pray this day for those searching for answers. Please be with those who are struggling in their faith, and help them to understand that you are with them always. So many people are in search of your love and everlasting grace. Please provide peace and comfort for those recovering from a loss of a loved one, loss of a job, or facing an illness, and with those dealing with anxiety, depression, and suicidal thoughts. I pray that all of your children understand they each have a purpose! Please continue to wrap your arms around us through our struggles and joys. You are our gracious, almighty Father who never fails in your plans for our lives. Amen.

~Pray and Give Thanks~

Personal Reflection . . .

_____

_____

_____

_____

_____

_____

_____

_____

Trust in the Lord with all thine heart; and lean not unto thine own understanding. (Proverbs 3:5 KJV)

♥Go to Him All You Broken-hearted♥

The Lord is nigh unto them that are of a broken heart; and saveth such as be of a contrite spirit. (Psalms 34:18 KJV)

Contrite means feeling or expressing remorse or penitence; affected by guilt. It means sorry, regretful, remorseful, and apologetic. So how are you doing today? I know many of you are recovering from the loss of a loved one, an illness, relationship struggles, parenting woes, job crises, or perhaps depression. Life just seems to stink sometimes, right?! Well, when scripture reassures us that we are to turn to God during these struggles, then we must do it. He's there to comfort us, to heal us, to love us and to reassure us that our pain is purely temporary. He's not going to mislead us! If anyone should be trusted, it's Him.

~He Will Always Heal Your Brokenness~

Personal Reflection . . .

_____

_____

_____

_____

_____

_____

_____

_____

_____

_____

_____

_____

Trust in the Lord with all thine heart; and lean not unto thine own understanding. (Proverbs 3:5 KJV)

♥Why So Much Doubt♥

Grace be unto you, and peace, from God our Father, and from the Lord Jesus Christ. I thank my God Always on your behalf, for the grace of God which is given you by Jesus Christ; that in everything ye are enriched by him, in all utterance, and in all knowledge; Even as the testimony of Christ was confirmed in you.
(1 Corinthians 1:3-6 KJV)

I'm seeing more and more hate speech on the Word of God every day. If you don't believe, why blaspheme His name? Why criticize those who choose to believe? I also see Christians using slander towards others as well. Why so much hate? This is one hundred percent the opposite of what we've been called to do! If you encounter someone with doubts and hate in their hearts, be patient. Let us be instructional and patient in our response to this negativity. It is NOT impossible to listen, love and educate those without faith. No Christian wants to be forced into not believing, just as non-Christians do not want to be forced into believing. If we are all brothers and sisters in Christ, let us start behaving as such. Let us listen to one another! Let us help to understand the importance of His Holy name and the wonders it brings to our lives!

~Let Us Be United in Christ~

Personal Reflection . . .

_____

_____

_____

_____

Trust in the Lord with all thine heart; and lean not unto thine own understanding. (Proverbs 3:5 KJV)

♥ Positivity Pays ♥

Let all bitterness and wrath and anger and clamor and slander be put away from you, along with all malice. Be kind to one another, tenderhearted, forgiving one another, as God in Christ forgave you. (Ephesians 4:31-32 ESV)

Don't hesitate to do what's right! Let go of your anger and wrath! When we are filled with hate, we leave very little room for love. But the Holy Spirit is upon us all, ready to guide us to a better place. We are NOT called to kill, steal, cheat, or lie. We are called to follow His Holy Word down a path of righteousness. Fill your mind with good thoughts, kind words, and happy moments. Everyone has the power to do this.

~Let Go of Hate, Open Your Heart to Love~

Personal Reflection . . .

_____
_____
_____
_____
_____
_____
_____
_____
_____
_____
_____
_____
_____
_____

Trust in the Lord with all thine heart; and lean not unto thine own understanding. (Proverbs 3:5 KJV)

❤There's Nothing Wrong with Saying We Are Wrong❤

If we confess our sins, he is faithful to forgive us our sins and to cleanse us from all unrighteousness. (1 John 1:9 ESV)

Committing sin is not to be taken lightly. If something is wrong, it's wrong. If something is right, it's right. The difference is admitting it to God. When you commit a wrong action in your relationships, do you apologize or make excuses for your wrong behavior? God has led us to obey his Commandments. If you have made mistakes, go to Him with a humble apology. If you sin against others, go to them with a humble apology. Don't make excuses for committing wrongful acts, God knows the truth anyway! Step up, be honest and sin no more.

~Confess Your Sins, Be Free~

Personal Reflection . . .

_____
_____
_____
_____
_____
_____
_____
_____
_____
_____
_____

Trust in the Lord with all thine heart; and lean not unto thine own understanding. (Proverbs 3:5 KJV)

♥*So Many People to Help*♥

But I have prayed for thee, that thy faith fail not: and when thou art converted, strengthen thy brethren (Luke 22:32-33 KJV)

You'll get a lot of "no's" but you'll also get a lot of yes's". When you come across those with little faith, don't turn away. This is when we must plant seeds. Those without faith often wonder why others have strong faith. They may disagree and have doubts but they are all worth sharing the Bible with. Everyone deserves to have Jesus in their life. Let us not turn away from those who become discouraged and weary. Let us build them up in the name of Christ! Start today and continue on this journey in the days ahead.

~Don't Give Up on Them~

Personal Reflection . . .

_____
_____
_____
_____
_____
_____
_____
_____
_____
_____
_____
_____

Trust in the Lord with all thine heart; and lean not unto thine own understanding. (Proverbs 3:5 KJV)

♥Choose to Find Joy in Your Journey♥

I think myself happy: because I shall answer for myself this day. (Acts 26:2 KJV)

When I take Jesus on my journey through life, the joy I feel brings me peace. I do not enjoy being in control, it causes my heart unnecessary stress. But knowing that He has the control, allows me to take a deep breath of relief.

I was recently told that someone close to me has trouble being around me because I'm too positive. To that I responded with a laugh! It's difficult being around people who wallow in self-pity and refuse to get out of their own state of victimization. I too have been there! But I chose to find the joy in my circumstances. It's a choice for everyone. Joy or wallow? I enjoy being positive, I enjoy being helpful, and I enjoy having Jesus as my center to keep me grounded. No matter what you're facing in life, there's no better feeling than being happy, smiling, and laughing! It's available for everyone.

~Joy, Journey, Jesus~

Personal Reflection . . .

_____

_____

_____

_____

_____

_____

_____

Trust in the Lord with all thine heart; and lean not unto thine own understanding. (Proverbs 3:5 KJV)

♥Thank You Jesus♥

For if we go on sinning deliberately after receiving the knowledge of the truth, there no longer remains a sacrifice for sins, but a fearful expectation of judgment. (Hebrews 10:26-27 ESV)

He sacrificed everything to save us. Let us think about how many times we sin. Is it daily, weekly, or more? We were saved once, but we must be mindful that it doesn't give us the excuse to continue sinning. We know right from wrong! So why is it easy sometimes to choose the wrong? The "wrong" thing is a temptation that we typically fall for on a daily basis. Let us not forget that we will still be judged. It's a scary thing to think about standing before our Lord and counting down how we have sinned and not turned to Him for instruction. What do our "sin lists" look like? It's not too late to repent and change. It's never too late to receive His mercy and grace.

~Sin is the Devil at Work, so Don't be Fooled by His Temptation~

Personal Reflection . . .

_____
_____
_____
_____
_____
_____
_____
_____

Trust in the Lord with all thine heart; and lean not unto thine own understanding. (Proverbs 3:5 KJV)

♥Have A Great Week♥

Praise the Lord! Praise God in His sanctuary; Praise Him in His mighty firmament! Let everything that hath breath praise the Lord. (Psalm 150:1-2,6 KJV)

Let us praise the Lord and have a positive week! Around our country many are experiencing high heat, wild fires, high humidity, and now more hurricanes. Let us continue to pray and work hard through these circumstances. For if we can continue to praise God, we can also continue to have a good week. The Lord is with us, let us celebrate! Let us rejoice, be happy and cast our worries unto Him, for He cares for us.

~Keep God Close to You and Have a Blessed Week~

Personal Reflection . . .

_____
_____
_____
_____
_____
_____
_____
_____
_____
_____
_____
_____
_____
_____

Trust in the Lord with all thine heart; and lean not unto thine own understanding. (Proverbs 3:5 KJV)

♥What's Up for Discussion♥

Whoever isolated himself seeks his own desire; he breaks out against all sound judgment. A fool takes no pleasure in understanding, but only in expressing his opinion...The words of a man's mouth are deep waters; the fountain of wisdom is a bubbling brook. It is not good to be partial to the wicked or to deprive the righteous of justice. (Proverbs 18:1-3 ESV)

Proverbs is intense but also speaks the truth! It's actually my favorite part of the Bible. Proverbs gives us two choices: right vs. wrong or good vs. evil. So, it's on my heart to talk about gossiping and being negative today. Where do we stand when we speak negatively of others? Whether it's our family, friends, strangers, co-workers, people in higher power, or God himself, it's wrong to gossip and slander others. If we want to educate those who offer opinions that differ from ours, then let's do it respectfully, fully aware that God sees and hears everything we say and do.

It's important to think about how you will feel after you say something negative. Are your words helpful, encouraging, and kind? Or are they hurtful, demeaning, and cowardly? If you're stuck in a situation where you're faced with confrontation or a temptation to gossip, first take a breath and remember that what you say can never be taken back. We are all better than the gossip and negativity we preach.

~Take a Step Back and Think about What's Right~

Trust in the Lord with all thine heart; and lean not unto thine own understanding. (Proverbs 3:5 KJV)

Personal Reflection . . .

_____

_____

_____

_____

_____

_____

_____

_____

_____

_____

_____

_____

_____

_____

_____

_____

_____

_____

_____

_____

_____

_____

_____

_____

_____

_____

_____

Trust in the Lord with all thine heart; and lean not unto thine own understanding. (Proverbs 3:5 KJV)

♥*Emptiness is an Outreach*♥

I have set the Lord always before me: because he is at my right hand, I shall not be moved. (Psalm 16:8 KJV)

Are you lonely? Feeling empty and uncertain? These emotions are highly typical for everyone, so please understand that you don't struggle alone. When these sensitive emotions take over, God knows. He sees everything we go through. I understand that many people wish that He could wave a magic wand and take it all away, but that's what our faith is for. We actually do have the power to improve our own situations. God won't force Himself into our lives; we must turn to Him for peace and understanding. He's there! He's waiting for your prayers, your communication, and your time to read His Word. He's there for you to trust and to love.

~Reach Out to Him, He'll Never Leave You or Forsake You~

Personal Reflection . . .

_____
_____
_____
_____
_____
_____
_____
_____
_____
_____

Trust in the Lord with all thine heart; and lean not unto thine own understanding. (Proverbs 3:5 KJV)

❤*Give Him All the Glory and Praise*❤

O give thanks unto the Lord, for he is good: for his mercy endureth forever. (Psalm 107:1 KJV)

There will be many times in our lives where giving thanks to God will naturally flow from our hearts. In fact, we should be able to thank Him every day.

Thank you, God, for a new day
Thank you for a new chance to be a better Christian
Thank you for loving me through my struggles
Thank you for my children, friends and pets
Thank you for your everlasting mercy and grace
Thank you for listening to the cries of my heart
Thank you for my family
Thank you for forgiving me when I have made mistakes
Thank you for guiding me down a path of helping others
receive your Word

~Thank You~

Personal Reflection . . .

_____
_____
_____
_____
_____
_____
_____
_____
_____

Trust in the Lord with all thine heart; and lean not unto thine own understanding. (Proverbs 3:5 KJV)

❤Christian In Training❤

Then Jesus told his disciples, "If anyone would come after me, let him deny himself and take up his cross and follow me."
(Matthew 16:24 ESV)

Is anyone perfect? No! We Christians are not perfect people, but we need to be Christians in training! We make mistakes, we perceive the meaning of scripture in different ways, and we also become discouraged. This is why God's Word is meant to guide our footsteps in the direction of Jesus. He is our constant reminder on how to live righteously. It is never too late for people to change! It is never too late to turn to Him for help! He IS help. He is our hope, our light, and our redeemer. Our darkness does not define us, but how we overcome the darkness does! Be a better Christian today than you were yesterday.

~ Focus on What is Right, What is Pure, and What is Good~

Personal Reflection . . .

Trust in the Lord with all thine heart; and lean not unto thine own understanding. (Proverbs 3:5 KJV)

♥ His Plans ♥

"For I know the plans I have for you," says the Lord. "Plans for good and not for disaster, to give you a future and a hope." (Jeremiah 29:11 NLT)

The plans we make will not typically be the same ones that He has for our lives. Have you tried different jobs that haven't worked in your favor? Or how about relationships and parenting techniques? Traveling through this life and trying to figure things out doesn't have to happen on our own. In fact, God's plans for us can be one hundred percent the opposite of what we want our own plans to be. I'm still in disbelief that I have four children! I thought about it and planned on only having two. My plan was to work with children until retirement. Then I started having severe back issues. Now I'm writing about God's Word (which I never planned on doing). Funny how God knows what's best for us, huh? It's funny how mysterious He is! My advice to you is to let God lead you. If you aren't sure how to do that, listen reflectively through prayer. Follow your heart out of pure love for something, not something you feel obligated to do.

~Be Ready for Him to Guide You to Something You Never Thought was Possible~

Personal Reflection . . .

_____

_____

_____

_____

_____

_____

Trust in the Lord with all thine heart; and lean not unto thine own understanding. (Proverbs 3:5 KJV)

♥You've Got This♥

I am leaving you with a gift, peace of mind and heart. And the peace I give is a gift the world cannot give. So don't be troubled or afraid. (John 14:27 NLT)

You will find peace in His Word! Why be filled with anxiety when you can be filled with the Holy Spirit? You don't have to have everything figured out; God doesn't expect you to. It's okay to stop and take a breath. It's okay to relax and rest in this demanding world. The pressure that humans put on themselves and others is not God's intention for our lives. You don't have to have everything figured out right now! You don't have to have all the answers! What you do have to have is faith and trust in God's plan.

~Don't Be Anxious, Trust in His Plan~

Personal Reflection . . .

_____
_____
_____
_____
_____
_____
_____
_____
_____
_____
_____
_____
_____

Trust in the Lord with all thine heart; and lean not unto thine own understanding. (Proverbs 3:5 KJV)

♥*Stress is The Devil's Smile*♥

Blessed is the man who remains steadfast under trial, for when he has stood the test, he will receive the crown of life, which God has promised to those who love him. (James 1:12 ESV)

He will always try to bring us down! The Devil, with his scandalous ways, wants nothing more than to break us from the hands of God. It's a trap; it always has been. Jesus was tempted for forty days and nights at the hand of Satan. But Jesus prevailed through prayer and fully understanding the promises of God. He trusted in His Holy Word and made an example for all of us to follow. Stress is a painstaking emotion that can quite literally destroy your body. Back pain, headaches, tears, shortness of breath, exhaustion, anxiety, chest pains, and joint pain, along with wanting to hide from family and friends, can all be the outcome of stress. I've experienced all of these. There is a solution! You can overcome stress with prayer and reminders of the wonderful blessings in your life. Your mindset can help you through your struggles. Write down your blessings and say them out loud. Hearing your own voice speak of positive things will make you smile. Try it!

~Blessings Are from God, Observe Them Daily~

Personal Reflection . . .

_____

_____

_____

_____

_____

_____

Trust in the Lord with all thine heart; and lean not unto thine own understanding. (Proverbs 3:5 KJV)

♥Always Find A Reason♥

Let your light shine before others, that they may see your good deeds and glorify your Father in Heaven. (Matthew 5:16 NIV)

Laughter, light, shine, glorify, life, good deeds, Heaven. Key words are important! In the Bible and in life, key words that guide us toward living out our best days are right in front of us. Never does the Scripture tell us to be discouraged, anxious, worried, afraid, angry, or annoyed. God knows what's best for us! Our family and friends should also guide us in a positive direction. If you're struggling to find a path to take or simply want joy in your life, turn to Him for guidance. Always find a reason to laugh, smile, love, give, be a blessing, and enjoy your days.

~Let Your Laughter Shine before Others~

Personal Reflection . . .

_____

_____

_____

_____

_____

_____

_____

_____

_____

_____

_____

_____

Trust in the Lord with all thine heart; and lean not unto thine own understanding. (Proverbs 3:5 KJV)

♥What Do You Fear♥

And he said, "my presence shall go with thee, and I will give thee rest." (Exodus 33:14 KJV)

"My presence shall go with thee, and I will give thee rest". God's Word gives comfort to those in need, guidance to those who are lost, and peace to those who are hopeless. Do you read His Word regularly? Seek Him in all you do. He wants us to go to Him. He wants us to praise His Holy name, which He deserves. Our Father, our creator, our redeemer.

~Allow Him in and You'll Be Free~

Personal Reflection . . .

_____
_____
_____
_____
_____
_____
_____
_____
_____
_____
_____
_____
_____
_____
_____
_____

Trust in the Lord with all thine heart; and lean not unto thine own understanding. (Proverbs 3:5 KJV)

♥*Commandments*♥

Therefore shall ye keep my commandments, and do them: I am the Lord. (Leviticus 22:31 KJV)

The commandments are a divine rule, and they are rules to be strictly observed. They are His rules for us to live by, just as we set rules and boundaries for our own children. They keep us safe, grounded and responsible. His purpose for our lives is for us to be honorable human beings who choose wisely when faced with obstacles in life. He is gracious with us in His reminders, which clearly come from His love.

The Ten Commandments
Thou shalt have no other gods before me;
Thou shalt not make unto thee any graven image;
Thou shalt not take the name of the Lord thy God in vain;
Remember the sabbath day, to keep it holy;
Honor thy father and thy mother;
Thou shalt not kill;
Thou shalt not commit adultery;
Thou shalt not steal;
Thou shalt not bear false witness against thy neighbor;
Thou shalt not covet thy neighbor's house, nor any thing that is thy neighbors. (KJV)

~Take His Commandments to Heart~

Trust in the Lord with all thine heart; and lean not unto thine own understanding. (Proverbs 3:5 KJV)

Personal Reflection . . .

Trust in the Lord with all thine heart; and lean not unto thine own understanding. (Proverbs 3:5 KJV)

❤Focus on the Beauty around You❤

The light is sweet, and it pleases the eyes to see the sun.
(Ecclesiastes 11:7 NIV)

Nature is full of wonder! How often do you take time to truly appreciate our world we live in? In the midst of hardships, there is always something beautiful to witness. Just driving six hours this morning to my family's home, I was able to enjoy the sunrise, a little rain, a rainbow, blue skies, mountains full of greenery, white clouds, and a cooler breeze. This has all been created by His marvelous hand. Take time to witness His great work!

~God's Creation Is All around Us~

Personal Reflection . . .

_____
_____
_____
_____
_____
_____
_____
_____
_____
_____
_____
_____
_____
_____

Trust in the Lord with all thine heart; and lean not unto thine own understanding. (Proverbs 3:5 KJV)

♥ *It's Healthy to Withdraw* ♥

But when you pray, go into your room and shut the door and pray to your Father who is in secret. And your Father who sees in secret will reward you. (Matthew 6:6 ESV)

How often do you take time to sit in silence? Time to relax, rest and speak to God? I know in a busy world it seems nearly impossible sometimes to take time for yourself, but it's a must to slow down! Set aside a small amount of time daily to withdraw to a quiet place, even for just ten minutes. Jesus often retreated to a place of quiet to speak to God from His heart. His example has taught us that we too need to quiet our minds and go to our Lord in silence. We all need and deserve peace in our hearts.

~Find a Quiet Place to Pray and Rest~

Personal Reflection . . .

_____

_____

_____

_____

_____

_____

_____

_____

_____

_____

_____

_____

Trust in the Lord with all thine heart; and lean not unto thine own understanding. (Proverbs 3:5 KJV)

♥Protect Our Fruit♥

Behold, children are a heritage from the Lord, the fruit of the womb a reward. (Psalm 127:3 ESV)

Protect our children, O Lord. We pray to you that you bless each and every child with good health, safety, and endless happiness. We fully understand that life will be challenging, but we have been commanded to trust in your Will for our lives. Today we ask that you please protect our children when we cannot. Please keep close watch over our schools, homes, and streets. Thank you for your endless love and comfort when our children have needed you and have felt alone in their own insecurities.

~ God Bless All of the Children~

Personal Reflection . . .

_____

_____

_____

_____

_____

_____

_____

_____

_____

_____

_____

_____

_____

_____

Trust in the Lord with all thine heart; and lean not unto thine own understanding. (Proverbs 3:5 KJV)

♥Come Boldly unto the Throne♥

Let us therefore come boldly unto the throne of grace, that we may obtain mercy, and find grace to help in time of need.
(Hebrews 4:16 KJV)

Good Morning! Let us give thanks and praise before heading out into our busy routines. God is shining His grace upon each and every one of us this fresh new week. There is so much to be happy about! Have you smiled yet this morning? Please do. Go out and do something kind for a stranger. Go out and share your joy. Go out and share God's Word! I pray that you all find peace in your work place, with parenting, in your home life, and during your new adventures. Know that our Lord is with you all.

~Many Blessings to Each and Every One of You~

Personal Reflection . . .

_____

_____

_____

_____

_____

_____

_____

_____

_____

_____

_____

_____

Trust in the Lord with all thine heart; and lean not unto thine own understanding. (Proverbs 3:5 KJV)

❤What Are You Smiling About❤

Those who look at Him are radiant, and their faces shall never be ashamed. (Psalm 34:5 ESV)

We each have something to smile about every single day! Let's all take a moment and smile at the fact that our God is amazingly wonderful. Thank you, God, for another morning, another day, another chance to do our best. Without you, all hope would be lost. Your love and mercy guide us, your children, to become better people in your Holy name. All of our praises and worship belong to your everlasting sovereign name. Thank you for all that you've done and all that you will continue to do!

~Smile to the Heavens and Have A Blessed Day~

Personal Reflection . . .

_____
_____
_____
_____
_____
_____
_____
_____
_____
_____
_____
_____
_____
_____

Trust in the Lord with all thine heart; and lean not unto thine own understanding. (Proverbs 3:5 KJV)

♥Every Day Counts♥

Therefore do not be anxious about tomorrow, for tomorrow will be anxious for itself. Sufficient for the day is its own trouble. (Matthew 6:34 ESV)

I love the thought of not being anxious today, but tomorrow there will be difficulties. It's taken me some thought and experience to understand what this means. It means that, for today, cast your anxieties and worries upon Him. Enjoy this day and do your best to try and not anticipate what tomorrow can bring. Then tomorrow do the same! Then, when the next day comes, continue to cast your anxiety unto Him. It's a pattern, and to do this, we must be in prayer daily, not just when we face difficulties.

~Do Not be Anxious~

Personal Reflection . . .

_____

_____

_____

_____

_____

_____

_____

_____

_____

_____

_____

Trust in the Lord with all thine heart; and lean not unto thine own understanding. (Proverbs 3:5 KJV)

♥Even at Your Lowest, Get Back Up♥

Be strong and courageous. Do not fear or be in dread of them, for it is the Lord your God who goes with you. He will not leave you or forsake you. (Deuteronomy 31:6 ESV)

Are you feeling like you're at your lowest? Sometimes I feel that things seem to add up and try to push me down. I've been through enough to know that staying defeated is NEVER an option. God is my strength! I remind myself to be strong in Him. If I told you how many times each day I talk to him as a friend and in prayer, you'd be shocked. But hey, I've come out stronger every time. We get choices in life. How do you choose to react when you "fall"? How do you respond to life's hardships? Your reaction means everything!

~God is with Us All~

Personal Reflection . . .

_____

_____

_____

_____

_____

_____

_____

_____

_____

_____

_____

_____

Trust in the Lord with all thine heart; and lean not unto thine own understanding. (Proverbs 3:5 KJV)

♥ *In Our Weaknesses* ♥

Likewise the Spirit helps us in our weakness. For we do not know what to pray for as we ought, but the Spirit himself intercedes for us with groanings too deep for words. (Romans 8:26 ESV)

There is no substitute for the Holy Spirit. It is in us and for us all. The Holy Spirit is the Spirit of God. It is God's power in action, His active force. The Holy Spirit is used in many different forms in the Bible. Have you felt the presence of it? Has it called you to your higher purpose? Have you turned to it in your time of need? His Spirit guides, protects, comforts and understands. It guides us through "right" and "wrong" moments in our life. The Holy Spirit will not prompt us to go against scripture. It is purely for our benefit. We must do our part to be good children of God and allow the Holy Spirit to lead us.

~There is No Substitute~

Personal Reflection . . .

_____
_____
_____
_____
_____
_____
_____
_____
_____
_____

Trust in the Lord with all thine heart; and lean not unto thine own understanding. (Proverbs 3:5 KJV)

❤Do You Know Someone❤

Do not grumble against one another, brothers, so that you may not be judged; behold, the Judge is standing at the door.
(James 5:9 ESV)

Do you know someone who constantly complains and is constantly negative? Or are you that type of person? It's no secret that being around negative people causes strain in a relationship. If we know someone who complains, do we therefore turn our backs and complain about them? It goes both ways. So, what is the best solution? Many of us distance ourselves and walk away from that type of person. Maybe we can remind them of their blessings daily? Or we can pray for them that they change? When I'm personally faced with negative people, I try and stay positive. I will listen, then offer advice, then pray for them. Remember how God said to pray for our enemies? I feel that this is the ultimate answer. BUT it doesn't mean that it's easy. People who complain are extremely difficult to be around. I have a few family members who are in a constant state of negativity. It saddens me, but I stay hopeful through prayer that they feel the Holy Spirit's positive influence. Let us all stop complaining and pray for those who need help the most!

~Don't Complain About the Complainers. Always Be A Positive Influence~

Trust in the Lord with all thine heart; and lean not unto thine own understanding. (Proverbs 3:5 KJV)

Personal Reflection . . .

Trust in the Lord with all thine heart; and lean not unto thine own understanding. (Proverbs 3:5 KJV)

♥You Deserve Your Best Life♥

And whenever you stand praying, forgive, if you have anything against anyone, so that your Father also who is in Heaven May forgive you your trespasses. (Mark 11:25 ESV)

I'll share with you how to forgive someone who has hurt you. I will share from my experience because you deserve to live in peace! I lived with uncertainty, fear, depression, and anger after my third child was born. I was working 10 to 12 hours a day running a preschool, mom of three, tons of bills to pay, and was confronted with my husband wanting a divorce (I will keep the reasons why private). My world came crashing down. In an instant everything I knew and trusted was gone. Looking back now I see it was a blessing in disguise, but of course I didn't see it that way at the time! Through those tough times I prayed, I continued to be the best mom and tried to keep a smile on my face. What I could not do was be nice to him or show any type of forgiveness. As I started rebuilding my life, like everyone should in tough times, I started to see that I was pretty darn strong and independent. But I also realized that the one thing I didn't want any more was the anger in my heart. I finally just looked up and said, "I forgive him God". And just like, that I felt a huge weight be lifted from my heart. I didn't even tell my ex-husband I forgave him; I told God! See, once you pray every day and turn your attention to a bigger power, things change in your life. I was able to live in peace. I felt God was proud of me for forgiving, and felt He was by my side and that everything was going to be okay. If you're struggling with forgiving someone, alive or deceased, look up say it out loud to God!

~Say it Today~

Trust in the Lord with all thine heart; and lean not unto thine own understanding. (Proverbs 3:5 KJV)

Personal Reflection . . .

Trust in the Lord with all thine heart; and lean not unto thine own understanding. (Proverbs 3:5 KJV)

♥Life Is Not Fair, But God Is Faithful♥

So we do not lose heart. Though our outer self is wasting away, our inner self is being renewed day by day. For this light momentary affliction is preparing for us an eternal weight of glory beyond all comparison, as we look not to the things that are seen but to the things that are unseen. For the things that are seen are transient, but the things that are unseen are eternal.
(2 Corinthians 4:16-18 ESV)

I don't think I even need to ask who thinks life has been unfair. We ALL have been through terribly difficult times that we just don't understand. But that's exactly what scripture says, doesn't it! Life is going to be hard and unfair at times. But what do we learn through these unfair times? Strength comes from facing difficulties along with acknowledging that we are not in control. Things will weigh us down to the darkest moments in life, BUT they won't take us away from His presence and love. He is eternal and our strong faith connects us to His glory. God has faith in us to stay strong through the hardships we face.

~We Can Pass any Test with His Support~

Personal Reflection . . .

_____

_____

_____

_____

_____

_____

_____

_____

Trust in the Lord with all thine heart; and lean not unto thine own understanding. (Proverbs 3:5 KJV)

♥Do You Ever♥

Therefore, confess your sins to one another and pray for one another, that you may be healed. The prayer of the righteous person has great power as it is working. (James 5:16 ESV)

Do you ever just look at someone and pray for them? We can and should pray for everyone we meet. Even strangers need and deserve prayers and blessings. When you find yourself caught up in your own stresses and anxieties, release these feelings by praying for others. It's a gift to give behind the scenes. When I'm driving, I look around at other cars and ask God to bless the people inside and their families. I pray for those walking on the sidewalks and entering into stores. Praying for others is contagious! Once you start praying for others, you'll find yourself doing it all the time. It is in the giving of prayer that we truly receive peace.

~Go Out and Pray for Others Today~

Personal Reflection . . .

_____

_____

_____

_____

_____

_____

_____

_____

_____

_____

Trust in the Lord with all thine heart; and lean not unto thine own understanding. (Proverbs 3:5 KJV)

♥There's A Difference♥

For "everyone who calls on the name of the Lord will be saved." (Romans 10:13 ESV)

God doesn't turn us away when we seek Him. We are the ones who turn Him away when He seeks us. See the difference? We will live a life of complaints and negativity if we continue to turn our backs on His love. It's there! It's always been there, but we live with free will to believe and live the way we desire. Ask yourself this honest question, "Am I living the best life I can live without Jesus?" I know many people try to, but I've seen so much unhappiness and uncertainty. I've learned that when I'm feeling lost and anxious, I don't have to go through it alone. I'm so sad for those who suffer inside and reject the idea of accepting His help. If you need proof that God heals, proof that He helps and proof that He loves you, here I am. I was uncertain and afraid, but found through prayer and scripture that, when I rely on Him, I can overcome anything. You can too!

~God Is for Us All~

Personal Reflection . . .

_____

_____

_____

_____

_____

_____

_____

_____

Trust in the Lord with all thine heart; and lean not unto thine own understanding. (Proverbs 3:5 KJV)

♥ *Never Say Never* ♥

Create in me a clean heart, O God, and renew a steadfast spirit within me. (Psalm 51:10 KJV)

It's never too late to renew your faith and it's never too late to start living your best life! Our best selves can be formed in the renewal of our loyalty to our Lord. This comes with peace, trust, hope, patience, understanding, friendship and eternal love. We learn about who we are when we look up more often. We learn and feel that there is so much more to live for when we focus on Him. For me personally, I lived a bitter and unsatisfied life for years. I allowed stress to take over on a daily basis and found myself praying for answers. I remember looking up and saying, "This can't be what you have planned for me. There has to be something more!" Well, there was more. Years later I find myself relating my experiences in life through God's Word to help others who have also struggled.

You have so much to give also! You can start living your best life, if you haven't already started. It doesn't take money, success or luck to do this. It takes faith and commitment.

~Follow Your Heart and He Will Lead You~

Personal Reflection . . .

_____

_____

_____

_____

_____

_____

Trust in the Lord with all thine heart; and lean not unto thine own understanding. (Proverbs 3:5 KJV)

♥Are You Aware♥

In him we have obtained an inheritance, having been predestined according to the purpose of him who works all things according to the counsel of his will. (Ephesians 1:11 ESV)

Are we truly stepping back and acknowledging what He has done for us? We cannot wait for perfect situations to feel gratitude. Life will be challenging on a daily basis, but don't let this stop you from seeing the blessings that surround you. If you need to take a step back, do it. If you need rest, take it. If you need Jesus in your life, open your Bible. If you need to be reminded of how wonderful your life is, look around you. Don't ever compare your life, body or feelings to anyone else's. God blesses us all differently.

~Be Aware of Your Blessings. Be Aware of how Fortunate You are~

Personal Reflection . . .

_____

_____

_____

_____

_____

_____

_____

_____

_____

_____

_____

Trust in the Lord with all thine heart; and lean not unto thine own understanding. (Proverbs 3:5 KJV)

♥*Pray for Your Enemies*♥

But I say to you, Love your enemies and pray for those who persecute you, so that you may be sons of your Father who is in heaven. (Matthew 5:44 ESV)

So many people live with hate in their hearts. Why? What good can possibly come from despising others? What positive outcome can come from gossiping, posting hate speech, or feelings of revenge, violence and hateful thinking? The answer is nothing. Nothing good comes out of this way of living. But what happens when we pray for those we dislike and disagree with? It doesn't just help them, it helps us! When we pray, we release those negative feelings to God, who is the one who can heal us and others who are hateful.

I started praying for my enemies and it was life changing. I have prayed for people I have never met but heard were violent and hateful from the news. I now pray for strangers when I'm out doing errands and ask God to bless them and their families. I pray that those who are filled with hate feel the Holy Spirit and change their negative ways. It's so easy!!! Praying for others and being kind doesn't cost anything but a few moments of your time.

~Pray for the Unjust to Change Their Ways~

Personal Reflection . . .

_____

_____

_____

_____

Trust in the Lord with all thine heart; and lean not unto thine own understanding. (Proverbs 3:5 KJV)

♥You Get To♥

Whatever you do, work heartily, as for the Lord and not for men. (Colossians 3:23 ESV)

What do you GET to do today? Work, parenting, vacation, rest, volunteer, housework, pay bills, exercise, eat healthy, be kind to others, go to church, play a sport, visit a doctor or hospital, or start something new? Our perception of life will determine how our days will run. The "I have to" vs. "I get to" is all about how you view your circumstances. Sometimes housework is repetitive and stressful. But it's an important part of life. When I clean and organize my home, I feel a huge sense of accomplishment. Just like when I'm doing my devotions! I don't "have to" share God's Word, I "get to" share His Word. Just this morning I'm taking my truck to the dealership because my AC broke in the 95-degree weather. I'm scared about how much it's going to cost to fix, but I'm also looking forward to getting it done. When we let our fears of the day get to us, it doesn't leave any room for the excitement we can encounter when accomplishing life's daily tasks. And it is exciting getting things done!

~Try Turning Your Mindset Around...Life Is Good~

Personal Reflection . . .

_____
_____
_____
_____
_____
_____

Trust in the Lord with all thine heart; and lean not unto thine own understanding. (Proverbs 3:5 KJV)

♥Relax, It's Your Time♥

And He said to them, "Come away by yourselves to a desolate place and rest a while." For many were coming and going, and they had no leisure even to eat. (Mark 6:31 ESV)

What are you full of? Our bodies and minds take on so much chaos in this world that it can be difficult to free ourselves from overthinking. Do you ever just say to yourself, "Okay, it's time to shut off the negativity and look up to the Heavens for peace"? Try it today. Go outside and just sit and listen to nature. Sit, look up and free your mind from the chaos. Just as children need their rest time, we adults need our quiet time, too. I look up to the trees and just stare with a quiet mind. I look, listen and breathe! Then I pray with an open heart and a trusting soul. It feels like that moment is a special bond between God and me. Everyone deserves to have that special bond with Him.

~Look Up, Listen, Breathe and Pray~

Personal Reflection . . .

_____

_____

_____

_____

_____

_____

_____

_____

_____

_____

Trust in the Lord with all thine heart; and lean not unto thine own understanding. (Proverbs 3:5 KJV)

♥ Hear My Cry ♥

Hear my cry, O God; attend unto my prayer. From the end of the earth will I cry unto thee, when my heart is overwhelmed: lead me to the rock that is higher than I. For thou hast been a shelter for me, and a strong tower from the enemy. I will abide in thy tabernacle forever: I will trust in the covert of thy wings. For thou, O God, hast heard my vows: thou hast given me the heritage of those that fear thy name. (Psalm 61:1-5 KJV)

Assurance, eternal protection, prayer, heart, lead me, shelter me, strong tower, abide, forever, trust, your wings and vows. These key words are just a few that describe what our Lord has to offer us in troubled times. When life gets you low, turn your eyes high to our Lord. Scripture wasn't written to help us sometimes; it was written to help us always. When you're suffering from living a life of sin, turn to His instruction to better yourself. Life can and will be difficult, BUT His grace and love are easy to obtain! They are there for you whenever you need them. Even those who detest His Word and live without faith can be loved and forgiven. "Here my cry, O God" is something we will all say if we haven't already. It's okay to be vulnerable to Him and it's okay to ask for His help.

~Assurance of God's Eternal Protection~

Personal Reflection . . .

_____

_____

_____

_____

_____

Trust in the Lord with all thine heart; and lean not unto thine own understanding. (Proverbs 3:5 KJV)

♥This Is Where I Get My Peace♥

Now the Lord of peace himself give you peace always by all means. The Lord be with you all. (2 Thessalonians 3:16 KJV)

It is the time to turn to our Lord. He is our God of Peace and through Him we will find salvation. If there's any advice I could give you today, it would be to go to Him in Love, repentance, and loyalty. You will never find one who loves you more than He. For He is the great I Am. Our Father, His Son and the Holy Spirit are with us always. Live in His peace when you struggle. Pray with a grateful and yearning heart daily.

~He is Waiting for You~

Personal Reflection . . .

_____

_____

_____

_____

_____

_____

_____

_____

_____

_____

_____

_____

_____

_____

_____

Trust in the Lord with all thine heart; and lean not unto thine own understanding. (Proverbs 3:5 KJV)

♥Conquer Your Anxiety and Worry♥

Do not be anxious about anything, but in everything by prayer and supplication with thanksgiving let your requests be made known to God. And the peace of God, which surpasses all understanding, will guard your hearts and minds in Christ Jesus.
(Philippians 4:6-7 ESV)

I can understand that it's becoming seemingly harder to live without worry and anxiety in our country. I wake up to it every morning. What causes this anxiety in my heart is seeing so much evil and hate consuming people we have been commanded to love. I can tell you that praying and trusting God helps. Are you living with anxiety? Are you living with worry on a regular basis? Whatever your reasons are for having these negative emotions, God sees and knows that you are struggling. Here are helpful ways to conquer your anxiety...

Breathe
Pray
Trust God
Read your Bible
Do something good for yourself and others
Exercise
Pray for your enemies
Love those around you
Pray some more
Look up and smile
Give thanks
Pray again
Clean your house, play with your kids

Trust in the Lord with all thine heart; and lean not unto thine own understanding. (Proverbs 3:5 KJV)

Humble yourselves, therefore, under the mighty hand of God so that at the proper time he may exalt you, casting all your anxieties on him, because he cares for you. (1 Peter 5:6-7 ESV)

Personal Reflection . . .

Trust in the Lord with all thine heart; and lean not unto thine own understanding. (Proverbs 3:5 KJV)

❤*Renew Your Soul*❤

And I will give you a new heart, and a new spirit I will put within you. And I will remove the heart of stone from your flesh and give you a heart of flesh. And I will put my spirit within you, and cause you to walk in my statutes and be careful to obey my rules. (Ezekiel 36:26-27 ESV)

No one is ever too far lost in sin to be saved! No one is ever too far lost in addiction to be saved! No one is ever too depressed, anxious or lonely to be saved! Everyone is worthy of receiving a fresh renewal of the Holy Spirit. Go to the Lord and seek His Word of encouragement. Seek His love and grace. Seek His commandments and apply them to your life. Seek Him always and find new strength.

~Our God Is an Awesome God~

Personal Reflection . . .

_____

_____

_____

_____

_____

_____

_____

_____

_____

_____

_____

_____

Trust in the Lord with all thine heart; and lean not unto thine own understanding. (Proverbs 3:5 KJV)

♥When Has He Strengthened You♥

God is our refuge and strength, an ever-lasting help in trouble. Therefore we will not fear, though the earth give way and the mountains fall into the heart of the sea, though its waters soar and foam and the mountains quake with their surging.
(Psalm 46:1-3 ESV)

He is our refuge and strength! He is our everlasting help in troubled times! When have you faced difficult times where you sought strength in our Lord?

I sought strength in God when I faced being a single mom of three young children. I didn't have any money, I lost my job, was going through a divorce and lived far from my family. I prayed and hoped for things to get better every day. Even through the depression, anxiety and uncertainty, I remained hopeful in my heart. God helped to keep me strong, brave and loyal to His great promises. Things did get better, and my faith will remain forever strong!

~His Strength Is Our Strength. We Need Only to Trust in Him Always~

Personal Reflection . . .

_____

_____

_____

_____

_____

_____

_____

Trust in the Lord with all thine heart; and lean not unto thine own understanding. (Proverbs 3:5 KJV)

♥Can You Do It♥

One gives freely, yet grows all the richer; another withholds what he should give, and only suffers want. Whoever brings blessing will be enriched, and one who waters with himself be watered. (Proverbs 11:24-25 ESV)

Kindness is the quality of being friendly, generous and considerate. It is affection, warmth, gentleness, concern and care. It is hard to believe that some people in our world aren't kind to others. Can you imagine being unkind? Can you admit that you've been unkind? It's never too late to change that! When you are kind, you can and will change someone's attitude. You will be remembered for your caring and warm nature. One who is kind is one who is honorable. Kindness creates peace not just for others but for ourselves.

~Be Kind Always~

Personal Reflection . . .

_____

_____

_____

_____

_____

_____

_____

_____

_____

_____

_____

Trust in the Lord with all thine heart; and lean not unto thine own understanding. (Proverbs 3:5 KJV)

♥*Be Strong in Your Example*♥

Don't let anyone look down on you because you are young. Set an example for the believers in what you say and in how you live. Also set an example in how you love and in what you believe. Show the believers how to be pure. (1 Timothy 4:12)

When you think about what you put out in this world, what does it look like? Do you lead or follow a bad crowd? Do you constantly sin where others are following your example? Or are you a positive leader or follower that sets an example of being kind, generous and loving? People of all ages watch what we do! Even those without faith can be changed by our positive example of living like Christ. I challenge you to write down how you interact with other people. Write down the positive and negative things you do and say. Be honest about it! It's okay to examine how we live and how we can become better.

~Your Example Is the Key to Changing Our World~

Personal Reflection . . .

_____

_____

_____

_____

_____

_____

_____

_____

_____

_____

Trust in the Lord with all thine heart; and lean not unto thine own understanding. (Proverbs 3:5 KJV)

♥Be Strong in Your Mind♥

Finally, my brothers and sisters, always think about what is true. Think about what is noble, right and pure. Think about what is lovely and worthy of respect. If anything is excellent or worthy of praise, think about those kinds of things. (Philippians 4:8 NIV)

Fill your mind with positive thoughts! If you see, read or experience a situation that creates anxiety and stress, go to God in prayer. Go to Him to release these thoughts that keep you from living a fulfilling day. Clean out your mind as you would clean out your closet full of clutter. Remove old ideas that take up too much space like you would remove old piles of shoes. Remove the negativity from your mind like removing old clothes that don't fit you anymore. Remove thoughts of regret, sadness and abuse like you would remove old clothes with holes in them. Having a closet full of old tattered and worn out clothes holds you back from wearing new clothes full of vibrant, cheerful colors! Replace the old negative thoughts of junk in your mind with new bright and cheerful positive thoughts.

~Create in Your Mind new Moments of Greatness~

Personal Reflection . . .

_____
_____
_____
_____
_____
_____
_____

Trust in the Lord with all thine heart; and lean not unto thine own understanding. (Proverbs 3:5 KJV)

♥Challenges Equal Growth♥

Because how I suffered for Christ, I'm glad that I am weak. I am glad in hard times. I am glad when people say mean things about me. I am glad when things are difficult. And I am glad when people make me suffer. When I am weak, I am strong. (2 Corinthians 12:10 NIV)

I am glad when I face challenges. As hard as they may seem sometimes, these challenges force me to turn to God in the best way possible! I turn to Him; I count on Him; and I become more aware of what I can handle. I grow, I learn and I conquer my strength physically, mentally, and spiritually. I am strong in God. I am strong in God's Word. I am strong in tough times.

~Grow in Your Challenges~

Personal Reflection . . .

Trust in the Lord with all thine heart; and lean not unto thine own understanding. (Proverbs 3:5 KJV)

♥Be Strong in God♥

Here is what I am commanding you to do, be strong and brave. Do not be afraid. Do not lose hope. I am the Lord your God and I will be with you everywhere you go. (Joshua 1:9 ESV)

I've recently had the privilege of guiding our church's basketball camp kids in Devotion time. Our theme was "Be Strong in God". What a fantastic reminder for us all! It's important for people of ALL ages to learn the importance of scripture and God's love for us. Through God we are physically, mentally and spiritually strong. Through exercising, healthy eating, reading and learning, along with prayer time, we thrive in His Holy name. Stay strong in the battles you face, because without these battles how do we ever learn the importance of staying strong.

~Be Strong in God Physically, Mentally and Spiritually~

Personal Reflection . . .

_____
_____
_____
_____
_____
_____
_____
_____
_____
_____
_____
_____
_____

Trust in the Lord with all thine heart; and lean not unto thine own understanding. (Proverbs 3:5 KJV)

♥Depend on the Lord♥

Finally, let the Lord make you strong. Depend on his mighty power. (Ephesians 6:10 ESV)

Through darkness and light, lean on Him.
Through good and bad, lean on Him.
Through jobs, parenting and anxiety and addiction, lean on Him.
Through illness, depression and loneliness, lean on Him.
Through joys, family time and celebration, lean on Him.

Our Father loves us with an everlasting love, with arms wide enough to hold us all. Enjoy this life you live with full awareness that He is by your side. For nothing can separate us from Him.

Personal Reflection . . .

_____
_____
_____
_____
_____
_____
_____
_____
_____
_____
_____
_____
_____

Trust in the Lord with all thine heart; and lean not unto thine own understanding. (Proverbs 3:5 KJV)

♥Freedom Is Ours♥

Everyone who makes a practice of sinning also practices lawlessness; sin is lawlessness. (1 John 3:4 ESV)

Through Him our souls are set free! Jesus has come to take away our sin. But let's first examine that sin is defined as an immoral act considered to be a transgression against Devine law. It is a wrong, a wrongdoing, an act of evil/wickedness, a crime and offense. We have been loved beyond measure by the one who was sent to rescue us. His blood washed away our sins. In return, we must obey our Lord's commandments and live well with one another. If you face sin and the Holy Spirit is telling you to walk away, listen and learn. We always have a choice to do the right thing!

~More Jesus, Less Sin~

Personal Reflection . . .

_____

_____

_____

_____

_____

_____

_____

_____

_____

_____

_____

_____

_____

Trust in the Lord with all thine heart; and lean not unto thine own understanding. (Proverbs 3:5 KJV)

♥ Hope Anchors Our Souls ♥

Now the God of hope fill you with all joy and peace in believing, that ye may abound in hope, through the power of the Holy Ghost. (Romans 15:13 KJV)

Hope keeps us grounded in the understanding that good things are to come. And good will come! Stay firm in your faith, humble in your ways, keep the ways of Jesus Christ, keep our Lord's commandments alive, and pray. Hope helps us turn to God when times get tough and this "hope" rejuvenates our souls.

I pray this day that you refocus your mind and heart mentally and spiritually toward your everlasting hope in God's promises. Hold onto it as you hold onto your children, full of love, compassion and thanksgiving.

~We Wait in Hope for the Lord~

Personal Reflection . . .

Trust in the Lord with all thine heart; and lean not unto thine own understanding. (Proverbs 3:5 KJV)

♥All Who Are Weary and Burdened♥

Come unto me, all ye that labour and are heavy laden, and I will give you rest. (Matthew 11:28-29 KJV)

"All" is defined as a whole quantity of a particular group or thing; everyone, everybody and each person. So, when Jesus says "come unto me, all ye that labour and are heavy laden", He means YOU. He means every single person. No man, woman, or child are excluded from His love.

Go to Him in prayer,
Go to Him with an open heart,
Go to Him in thanksgiving and gratitude,
Go to Him in understanding,
Go to Him today.

Personal Reflection . . .

_____

_____

_____

_____

_____

_____

_____

_____

_____

_____

_____

_____

_____

Trust in the Lord with all thine heart; and lean not unto thine own understanding. (Proverbs 3:5 KJV)

♥Revive Me According to Your Word♥

Consider mine affliction, and deliver me: for I do not forget thy law. Plead my cause, and deliver me: quicken me according to thy word. (Psalm 119:153-154 KJV)

Studying scripture is important. With education comes understanding. With understanding comes patience. With patience comes faith. With faith all things are possible. "Great are your tender mercies, O Lord". These are not just words for some people, these are words for everyone to abide by. Everyone is welcome! Even those who lead a life of sin can change and be reborn. The glory that awaits you is unmeasurable! Turn from your doubt and grow in our Lord's love. Doubt is a sword that pierces our minds, allowing us to believe that nothing good can come our way. But when we understand that He is the way, all that is left in our hearts is love.

~Prepare Your Heart for His Word~

Personal Reflection . . .

_____
_____
_____
_____
_____
_____
_____
_____
_____
_____

Trust in the Lord with all thine heart; and lean not unto thine own understanding. (Proverbs 3:5 KJV)

❤Wait in Hope for the Lord❤

Rejoice in hope, be patient in tribulation, be constant in prayer. (Romans 12:12 ESV)

Turning to scripture brings so much peace to my soul. I'm waking this morning overwhelmed with anxiety and negative emotions due to the constant upheaval in our world. You know the saying, "don't take the world's problems on your shoulders"? Well don't! This is why we have been told to cast our cares and worries unto Him. He brings peace to our worries! If you're struggling today, my recommendation to you is this – turn OFF any social media and news that destroys your peace. Pray and be patient while waiting for relief. Keep yourself busy doing something positive! Spend time with those who bring you joy and do the best you can at your job.

~Hope, Patience and Prayer~

Personal Reflection . . .

_____
_____
_____
_____
_____
_____
_____
_____
_____
_____
_____
_____

Trust in the Lord with all thine heart; and lean not unto thine own understanding. (Proverbs 3:5 KJV)

❤*Take Nothing for Granted*❤

Love never gives up. (1 Corinthians 13:7 NLT)

Love never gives up and neither will those special moments in life. Memories fill our hearts when sadness seems to take over. Our minds are like eagles soaring through the wind. We have been blessed with moments that make us smile, laugh and create relationships with those we cannot see. I've lived far away from family for 14 years, but the memories we make each time we get together are irreplaceable. Which moments bring you joy? Which moments create peace in your life?

~Don't Count the Days, Make the Days Count~

Personal Reflection . . .

_____
_____
_____
_____
_____
_____
_____
_____
_____
_____
_____
_____
_____
_____

Trust in the Lord with all thine heart; and lean not unto thine own understanding. (Proverbs 3:5 KJV)

♥Do You Ever♥

Who saved us and called us to a Holy calling, not because of our works but because of his own purpose and grace, which he gave us in Christ Jesus before the ages began. (2 Timothy 1:9 ESV)

Do you ever wonder what God wants of you?
Do you ever think about Him and His plan for your life?
Do you ever speak out loud to Him?
Do you ever pray for guidance?
Do you ever just sit in quiet?
Do you ever wonder what it would be like to hear your calling?
Do you ever?

You will hear it if you haven't already! Are you ready to receive it? Are you ready to quiet your mind and hear it? Or maybe you've heard it and pushed it aside? We all have a purpose according to His plan. Not our plan, His plan! Wherever you are in life, it's not too late to accept Christ as your savior. It's not too late to hear His calling to better your life and the lives of those around you. You need only to be still and listen.

Personal Reflection . . .

_____

_____

_____

_____

_____

_____

_____

_____

Trust in the Lord with all thine heart; and lean not unto thine own understanding. (Proverbs 3:5 KJV)

♥*Good Morning*♥

I have come into the world as light, so that whoever believes in me may not remain in darkness (John 12:46 ESV)

What a way to brighten your day! To know that He has come to save us from darkness. If this isn't good news then I'm not sure what is. I personally start each morning with a cup of coffee and writing a devotion. Of course, I have to throw in my four kids already asking for something or being loud, but hey that's my life. How do you wake up? Are you waking up in the light or are you already dreading that the day will be dark? I too dread the mornings sometimes. That is until I start writing about God. He is an instant mood changer! Through Him I rediscover my hope for a brighter day! When you savor each sip of coffee and feel it bringing you to life, just remember that Jesus does the same. He heals, He loves, He saves. So, as you're enjoying your morning coffee each day, just know that Jesus also brings joy to your life.

~Sometimes all you need is a little bit of coffee and a whole lot of Jesus~

Personal Reflection . . .

_____

_____

_____

_____

_____

_____

_____

_____

Trust in the Lord with all thine heart; and lean not unto thine own understanding. (Proverbs 3:5 KJV)

♥How Is God Working through You♥

Truly, truly, I say to you, whoever believes in me will also do the works that I do; and greater works than these will he do, because I am going to the Father. (John 14:12 ESV)

When we place our faith in Christ, our life instantly changes. We have a greater idea of who He is and what He does. And as you acknowledge the great works of Christ, just imagine what God is capable of! He can and will work wonders through you. Maybe He already has and you have yet to recognize it? We have the power and privilege of being His peacekeepers here on earth. When we encourage others to do the right thing, speak only kind and understanding words, and share our joy, through us others will see Him.

~Love is the ultimate gateway when helping others understand who He is~

Personal Reflection . . .

_____
_____
_____
_____
_____
_____
_____
_____
_____
_____
_____
_____

Trust in the Lord with all thine heart; and lean not unto thine own understanding. (Proverbs 3:5 KJV)

❤ Just Keep Moving ❤

Beloved, I pray that all may go well with you and that you may be in good health, as it goes well with your soul. (3 John 1:2 ESV)

Don't get stuck, get active! Get up and move. Add some spontaneous motion to your days that can seem repetitive. Get your heartrate up, get a smile on your face, and put a little joy in your day. When you sit for too long, you start to feel lethargic and uninterested in things around you. You overthink and begin to make excuses for not having any energy. Why not let the love of God take over and encourage you to just keep moving. There is so much joy and so many rewards in taking care of yourself.

~Put a Little Step in Your Daily Routine~

Personal Reflection . . .

_____
_____
_____
_____
_____
_____
_____
_____
_____
_____
_____
_____

Trust in the Lord with all thine heart; and lean not unto thine own understanding. (Proverbs 3:5 KJV)

♥Quitting Should Never Be an Option♥

Seek the Lord and his strength; seek his face always.
(Psalm 105:4 CSB)

If you've thought about giving up, don't! Quitting is the easy thing to do, and yes, staying strong is difficult. The only difference is that staying strong moves you ahead in life. Why should you quit when God has given you the tools to get through your struggles? When faced with an illness, loneliness, bullying, depression, divorce, or loss of loved ones, I can completely understand how this would discourage you from pushing through to the next day. But are you struggling alone or are you turning to our Lord for help?

I've struggled alone before. It felt like torture! I was alone with three small children, no money or job, and I could barely afford groceries. I lost my grandmother at the same time, and I was struggling with depression. Thinking back on this reminds me of the darkness I lived in. BUT I also remember praying on a regular basis. Through prayer I felt hope—hope for better things to come. And better things eventually came! I did what any mom would do in hard times. I placed my focus on my children, my health, and God while waiting for things to improve. I fought back against depression and loneliness by starting my own in-home business. God placed a man in my life that changed everything, and he became an awesome stepdad. So, while things may seem impossible for you at this moment, it doesn't mean that you won't experience God's good grace!

~Keep Fighting, Stay Strong and Pray~

Trust in the Lord with all thine heart; and lean not unto thine own understanding. (Proverbs 3:5 KJV)

Personal Reflection . . .

_____

_____

_____

_____

_____

_____

_____

_____

_____

_____

_____

_____

_____

_____

_____

_____

_____

_____

_____

_____

_____

_____

_____

_____

_____

_____

_____

_____

Trust in the Lord with all thine heart; and lean not unto thine own understanding. (Proverbs 3:5 KJV)

❤With Age Comes Wisdom❤

With the ancient is wisdom; and in length of days
understanding. (Job 12:12 ESV)

If you are not familiar with the story of Job, I encourage you to read it. He was a loyal servant of God who faced severe challenges on earth. Loss of family, loss of land, loss of livestock and so on. Yet through it all he remained in God's favor. For no task the Devil laid before him could stop his love for the Lord. He was wise to know that God loved him and that holding onto his faith would create a path of righteousness. Learning from his story offers a new hope for how we live our lives. His faith, even in his old age, teaches us that it is never too late to place our trust and faith in God.

~I would rather be a servant of God than a prisoner of earth~

Personal Reflection . . .

_____
_____
_____
_____
_____
_____
_____
_____
_____
_____
_____
_____

Trust in the Lord with all thine heart; and lean not unto thine own understanding. (Proverbs 3:5 KJV)

♥The Simple Life♥

For our boast is this, the testimony of our conscience, that we behaved in the world with simplicity and godly sincerity, not by earthly wisdom but by the grace of God, and supremely so toward you. (2 Corinthians 1:12 ESV)

No one should be so overly stressed that they cannot see the beauty right in front of them. Blessings are a gift, so be sure to take note of them daily. Do not get so caught up in the "full steam ahead" aspects of life that you forget to give thanks. If you want and need to slow down, then do it! It's okay to simplify your life by letting go of any negativity holding you down. God wants to be a part of our lives. It's easy to leave Him out when we get busy. It's easy to forget Him when we hold onto negative thinking. When you become frustrated, just slow down, stop everything you're doing, and pray. By simplifying your life you're opening up room for God to be present.

~A Simpler Life Might be What You Need~

Personal Reflection . . .

_____

_____

_____

_____

_____

_____

_____

_____

_____

Trust in the Lord with all thine heart; and lean not unto thine own understanding. (Proverbs 3:5 KJV)

♥*Always Give Thanks and Praise*♥

When the righteous cry for help, the Lord hears and delivers them out of all their troubles (Psalm 34:17 ESV)

Dear Heavenly Father,

Thank you for allowing me to hit rock bottom so that I could build myself back up. Thank you for staying with me during my toughest hardships that I have faced. And thank you for blessing me with the ability to stay strong and positive. I truly have come out of the darkness as a child of faith, love, compassion, and most of all forgiveness. My life has been touched by Your mercy and grace. And even though I still struggle with sin, I pray that you continue to guide and mold me into the Christian you need me to be. Please help me to be the light that shines before others, so that through me they see you. In Jesus name I pray. Amen

Personal Reflection . . .

_____

_____

_____

_____

_____

_____

_____

_____

_____

_____

_____

_____

_____

Trust in the Lord with all thine heart; and lean not unto thine own understanding. (Proverbs 3:5 KJV)

❤*God Believes in You*❤

For the Lord will be your confidence and will keep your foot from being caught. (Proverbs 3:26 ESV)

If God believes in you then you can believe in yourself! We are not given this life to fear, we are given this life to live in joy. We are given the confidence to trust that He is with us to guide our steps. Take Him with you on your journey! Take Him with you to lean on in difficult situations. And take Him with you as a reminder that you are unstoppable with Him by your side. Your success, your perseverance and your faith are all His glory. Be humble on the path you take and you will go far.

~It takes several small footsteps to make one big imprint~

Personal Reflection . . .

_____
_____
_____
_____
_____
_____
_____
_____
_____
_____
_____
_____
_____
_____

Trust in the Lord with all thine heart; and lean not unto thine own understanding. (Proverbs 3:5 KJV)

♥*Yes You Can*♥

I can do all things through Christ which strengthens me.
(Philippians 4:13 KJV)

Just these few words in scripture provide so much power! Can you just imagine what your life would be like if you just shoved fear out of your way and pursued your dreams? If you get told no, even if you are ignored sometimes, you have the power to keep going! God has given you this power to make your life amazing. Honestly, the only person that ever stands in our way is the Devil. He's sneaks into our minds, trying to convince us that we aren't good enough. He tells us to quit! Why on earth would we ever quit when our Lord is telling us He is with us! He never leaves us! We have strength in Him to push forward.

~Just say No to Satan and say Yes to Jesus~

Personal Reflection . . .

Trust in the Lord with all thine heart; and lean not unto thine own understanding. (Proverbs 3:5 KJV)

♥ Shutting Off the Overthinking ♥

In peace I will lie down and sleep; for you alone, O Lord, make me dwell in safety. (Psalm 4:8 ESV)

Have you found that praying helps you overcome the unnecessary thoughts that keep you awake? If so, are you able and willing to share what helps you with others? It's hard to imagine the millions of people who suffer from lack of sleep due to overthinking. I personally pray and sleep with my Bible at night. This has created a blanket of peace and protection over me as I keep God close. I have welcomed Him in to take over the unnecessary anxiety I hold onto. Sharing the idea of prayer with those who don't typically pray can help them a great deal! It's through prayer that we relinquish what we cannot control and ask the one who can control it to take it from us. Just having Him to which we can express this is reassurance that we don't have to suffer alone.

~Pray before you Overthink~

Personal Reflection . . .

_____

_____

_____

_____

_____

_____

_____

_____

_____

Trust in the Lord with all thine heart; and lean not unto thine own understanding. (Proverbs 3:5 KJV)

♥ Reach Out to A Helpless Soul ♥

Put on then, as God's chosen ones, holy and beloved, compassionate hearts, kindness, humility, meekness, and patience. (Colossians 3:12 ESV)

Our lives are not shaped by how much we have. They are shaped by how much we give. Compassion means having sympathetic pity and concern for the sufferings or misfortunes of others. Jesus taught us about being compassionate toward others. It's not all about giving money, it's more about giving your time and kindness to helping others who struggle. When we listen, give advice, hug and just be there for someone who feels hopeless, we are being a blessing to their needs. Think about any family members, friends, coworkers or even strangers you've encountered that you can help today.

~Compassion is the Doorway to Healing a Hopeless Soul~

Personal Reflection . . .

Trust in the Lord with all thine heart; and lean not unto thine own understanding. (Proverbs 3:5 KJV)

♥*Please Do Not Let Fear Stop You*♥

Anxiety in a man's heart weighs him down, but a good word makes him glad. (Proverbs 12:25 ESV)

Fear is poison to the minds and hearts of people. It's a debilitating emotion that tries to convince us that we aren't good enough to achieve success. Fear is an earthly emotion created by the Devil. He will try anything to keep us from moving forward in a path of righteousness! During these times of fear, turn to scripture. God's Word is alive and exists purely for our benefit. We are reminded through His Word that fear is simple to overcome. Place your anxiety and insecurities of failing into our Lord's hands. Once you understand that He is on your side and not against you, you can achieve anything! Have a blessed successful day!

~Say No to Fear and Yes to Success~

Personal Reflection . . .

_____
_____
_____
_____
_____
_____
_____
_____
_____
_____
_____
_____

Trust in the Lord with all thine heart; and lean not unto thine own understanding. (Proverbs 3:5 KJV)

♥ People See Him through Us ♥

I press toward the mark for the prize of the high calling of God in Christ Jesus. (Philippians 3:14 KJV)

Are you acting justly as a child of God outside of church? Church can be a wonderful place of worship, but going out into the world as an individual child of God is a true calling. We should never just gather in a place of worship to share His good Word; we need to act as righteous Christians on behalf of His name everywhere we go! People see Him through us. Live well knowing you are kind and forgiving of others. Live well knowing He relies on you to share His Word. And live well knowing He is with you every step of the way on your journey.

~Go out and be a True Representation of His Word~

Personal Reflection . . .

_____
_____
_____
_____
_____
_____
_____
_____
_____
_____
_____
_____
_____
_____

Trust in the Lord with all thine heart; and lean not unto thine own understanding. (Proverbs 3:5 KJV)

♥*Stand Up for Your Faith*♥

It is God that girdeth me with strength, and maketh my way perfect. He maketh my feet like hinds' feet, and setteth me upon my high places. He teacheth my hands to war, so that a bow of steel is broken by mine arms. Thou hast also given me the shield of thy salvation: and thy right hand Holden me up, and thy gentleness hath made me great. (Psalm 18:32-35 KJV)

Having a positive influence means having the capacity to have an effect on the character, development, or behavior of someone or something. Influence means to have an impact. What kind of positive influence do you have on others? What do you want to be remembered for? No matter what you have done in your life, you can always turn it around to be an extraordinary child of God! Through Him we can build up our faith and share His love to the world.

~ His truth, His grace, His mercy and His home are all yours~

Personal Reflection . . .

_____

_____

_____

_____

_____

_____

_____

_____

_____

_____

Trust in the Lord with all thine heart; and lean not unto thine own understanding. (Proverbs 3:5 KJV)

♥Anytime♥

Let us search and try our ways, and turn again to the Lord. Let us lift up our heart with our hands unto God in the heavens. (Lamentations 3:40-41 KJV)

Freedom is a powerful thing. What do you do with your freedom? Don't ever let anyone tell you that you cannot pray or love God in your free time! The Free Will we have been given is a gift. It's a chance to get to know our Lord on our own. God doesn't want us to be forced to love Him, He wants us to go to Him out of love and devotion. Read scripture on your own, pray in every situation and go to God anytime.

~ The Greatest Freedom we have is to go to God at any Time~

Personal Reflection . . .

_____
_____
_____
_____
_____
_____
_____
_____
_____
_____
_____
_____
_____
_____
_____

Trust in the Lord with all thine heart; and lean not unto thine own understanding. (Proverbs 3:5 KJV)

♥*Blessed Are the Women on Earth*♥

An excellent wife who can find? She is far more precious than jewels. The heart of her husband trusts in her, and he will have no lack of gain. She does him good, and not harm, all the days of her life. (Proverbs 31:10-12 ESV)

What is our world without women? What is a marriage without her? The wisdom granted to each of us to raise a family and to work hard with our hands is to be appreciated and cherished. With a woman's love there isn't anything a family cannot handle. Pray for the women in your life. Hold them often with loving arms. Support them through difficult hardships. Tell them they are loved daily.

~Many Blessings Today and Every Day to the Women of God~

Personal Reflection . . .

_____

_____

_____

_____

_____

_____

_____

_____

_____

_____

_____

Trust in the Lord with all thine heart; and lean not unto thine own understanding. (Proverbs 3:5 KJV)

♥What is Making You Happy Today♥

Wake up, give thanks, and be happy! It's just that simple to do! Things to remember throughout your day...

Did I say thank you?
Did I pray?
Did I smile?
Did I hug my kids, pets or spouse?
Did I compliment someone?
Did I help someone?
Did I complain?
Did I share negative comments and behavior?
Did I stay calm in a tense situation?

~Happiness is obtained by controlling your thoughts, words and actions. So be sure to smile more often, laugh once a day and be kind always~

Personal Reflection . . .

_____
_____
_____
_____
_____
_____
_____
_____
_____
_____
_____
_____

Trust in the Lord with all thine heart; and lean not unto thine own understanding. (Proverbs 3:5 KJV)

♥Above All, Place Your Trust in God♥

Blessed is the man who trusts in the Lord, whose trust is the Lord. (Jeremiah 17:7 ESV)

Trust, faith, and hope are all yours! Let scripture be your guide. Let Jesus be present in your doubts and fears.

For in this hope we were saved. Now hope that is seen is not hope. For who hopes for what he sees? (Romans 8:24 ESV)

Go to Him in prayer, in thanksgiving, in sorrow, and in joy. Go to Him in love and in anger. His love for you is eternal, never to be forgotten or taken for granted.

Personal Reflection . . .

_____
_____
_____
_____
_____
_____
_____
_____
_____
_____
_____
_____
_____
_____
_____

Trust in the Lord with all thine heart; and lean not unto thine own understanding. (Proverbs 3:5 KJV)

♥Acceptance, Love and Wisdom♥

Pay careful attention to yourselves and to all the flock, in which the Holy Spirit has made you overseers, to care for the church of God, which he obtained with his own blood. (Acts 20:28 ESV)

Where do you belong? Where do you feel unconditional love and acceptance? Where are you filled with the wisdom of scripture? Where do you learn how to go out into the world and follow in the footsteps of Jesus? The church is a powerful place of worship. But which church best suits the needs of your heart? After years of longing to find the right one for me and my children, I was invited by a close friend to what is now a church I call home. Do not ever give up on seeking out what's best for you. We all have a special place in this world! We are all called for a special purpose!

~We are Called to Gather to Hear the Word of God~

Personal Reflection . . .

_____

_____

_____

_____

_____

_____

_____

_____

_____

_____

Trust in the Lord with all thine heart; and lean not unto thine own understanding. (Proverbs 3:5 KJV)

♥ Stand Up for Jesus ♥

Be sober-minded; be watchful. Your adversary the devil prowls around like a roaring lion, seeking someone to devour.
(1 Peter 5:8 ESV)

He stood up for us, all of us! We have been forgiven, guided, and given His everlasting grace. Now is the time to repent and to do what's right. Our world needs Jesus now more than ever. The Devil is mischievous and sneaks into our bodies and minds to take over and create unnecessary hate and violence. This hate can be overcome by turning our attention to Our Lord! Let us all look up in prayer. Let us all be kind to, forgiving of, and loving of our neighbors! Loving and forgiving those we dislike and disagree with is the best way to start.

~Start this day by forgiving those whom you are in opposition with. It's the right thing to do. ~

Personal Reflection . . .

_____
_____
_____
_____
_____
_____
_____
_____
_____
_____
_____
_____

Trust in the Lord with all thine heart; and lean not unto thine own understanding. (Proverbs 3:5 KJV)

♥You Are Worth Far More Than Your Possessions♥

Keep your life free from the love of money, and be content with what you have, for he has said, "I will never leave you nor forsake you". (Hebrews 13:5 ESV)

Worthy is defined as having adequate or great merit; character, or value. We were all created equal in the eyes of our Lord. Every single person has value. Do not allow your earthly possessions or other people define who you are! Let God do His job as our Father. Let Him love you, guide you and cherish you. It is no secret that some people will make you feel unworthy, unloved and undervalued. Do not give them this power over your life! It's important to remember that we are all unique, and when we can rise above the negativity, we can be who we were created to be. Let go of the idea of wanting more stuff and accept the fact that possessions and negative people are all temporary in this life.

~Grow from being the kind, humble person God has chosen you to be~

Personal Reflection . . .

_____
_____
_____
_____
_____
_____
_____
_____

Trust in the Lord with all thine heart; and lean not unto thine own understanding. (Proverbs 3:5 KJV)

♥ No One Is Ever Abandoned ♥

It is the Lord who goes before you. He will be with you; he will not leave you or forsake you. Do not fear or be dismayed. (Deuteronomy 31:8 ESV)

How far have you come? No matter where you are on your journey, continue to fight and stay strong. Strength comes from keeping hope in your heart! Hope comes from acknowledging that you want better and brighter days filled with joy! Joy comes from praying and keeping God close to you! And God is with you always. Typically, when we face giants in our lives and struggles that seem impossible to conquer, we tend to become exhausted. Rightfully so, as we are only human after all. But what we can gain from facing these giants is knowing that God is fighting with us and giving us the courage to keep on fighting.

~Keep going! Keep fighting! Keep humility and kindness alive! God is with you~

Personal Reflection . . .

_____
_____
_____
_____
_____
_____
_____
_____
_____
_____
_____

Trust in the Lord with all thine heart; and lean not unto thine own understanding. (Proverbs 3:5 KJV)

♥Pray for Everyone♥

Therefore, confess your sins to one another and pray for one another, that you may be healed. The prayer of a righteous person has great power as it is working. (James 5:16 ESV)

Let's all pray for others as we pray for ourselves. You'll find that praying for strangers and people you may dislike will bring a rewarding amount of peace to your heart. Instead of holding onto anger and bitterness toward those you disagree with, say a heartfelt prayer for them! Everyone is worthy of prayer. Everyone deserves your good, positive thoughts and well wishes. You also deserve to live with love for others in your heart.

~Prayer is like a best friend, it's always there for you when you need it~

Personal Reflection . . .

Trust in the Lord with all thine heart; and lean not unto thine own understanding. (Proverbs 3:5 KJV)

♥ Rise and Shine ♥

Arise, shine, for your light has come, and the glory of the Lord has risen upon you. (Isaiah 60:1 ESV)

Rise, shine and rejoice in this new day! It has been laid out before you. Be guided by the Holy Spirit and make the best decisions you can. Be humble and kind. Work hard, but also laugh. Do not be overcome by stress and anxiety, but control only what you can and give the rest to God. Make peace with others, not war. Help someone in need and never forget how important you are. When you rise, remember that you have purpose. When you shine, do it with class and dignity.

~Your Time is Now to Shine in a Positive Way~

Personal Reflection . . .

_____
_____
_____
_____
_____
_____
_____
_____
_____
_____
_____
_____
_____
_____
_____

Trust in the Lord with all thine heart; and lean not unto thine own understanding. (Proverbs 3:5 KJV)

♥ Remain Calm and Pray ♥

Draw nigh to God, and he will draw nigh to you. (James 4:8 KJV)

When your heart and mind are unsettled, please go to God in prayer. Overreacting in tense and stressful situations only causes anxiety. Keep your character and class in tact by remaining calm. Think before reacting, pray before reacting, and keep God as your center. Peace will only ever be achieved by putting your most positive self out into the world. Saying derogatory and inappropriate things will only come to hurt you in the end. Be mindful of others feelings. Be brave enough to remain calm and be the Christian God has called you to be.

~One of the Best Lessons in Life is how to Master Remaining Calm~

Personal Reflection . . .

_____
_____
_____
_____
_____
_____
_____
_____
_____
_____
_____
_____

Trust in the Lord with all thine heart; and lean not unto thine own understanding. (Proverbs 3:5 KJV)

❤*Let's Talk More about Trust*❤

The Lord is my strength and my shield; in Him my heart trusts, and I am helped; my heart exults, and with my song I give thanks to him. (Psalm 28:7 ESV)

Is there someone in your life that you trust in 100%? Someone who would never hurt you, lie to you, leave you, not love you, or betray you? I have one being that I trust every single day, even throughout my toughest challenges. There is no substitute for placing our trust in our Lord. He reminds us through scripture that He wants us to place our trust in Him always. What's keeping people from doing this? It brings great relief to my heart when I pray to Him and place my trust in Him. I also pray that others go to Him for relief and protection.

~I pray that you place your trust in our Lord~

Personal Reflection . . .

_____
_____
_____
_____
_____
_____
_____
_____
_____
_____
_____
_____

Trust in the Lord with all thine heart; and lean not unto thine own understanding. (Proverbs 3:5 KJV)

♥A Letter to Our Children♥

All your children shall be taught by the Lord, and great shall be the peace of your children. (Isaiah 54:13 ESV)

As you grow, remember to stay humble and kind.
Pray every day in the good times and in your troubled times.
Serve others over serving yourselves.
Share the Word of God with respect, truth and guidance.
Always think to yourselves, "What would Jesus do?"
Find happiness even when you're struggling.
Never ever take your family and blessings for granted.
Don't continue to want more stuff in life, but instead want more of Jesus.
Smile every chance you get.
Show love to others even if you are living with a broken heart.
Don't ever stay angry, instead be honest and truthful.
Learn and grow from your mistakes.
Always know that you are loved. Loved by God and loved by us.
There is greatness in each of you; be brave and dare to find out what it is.
You are our hearts. You are our souls. You are our purpose.

Love,

Your Parents

Trust in the Lord with all thine heart; and lean not unto thine own understanding. (Proverbs 3:5 KJV)

Personal Reflection . . .

Trust in the Lord with all thine heart; and lean not unto thine own understanding. (Proverbs 3:5 KJV)

♥ Trust ♥

Be still, and know that I am God. I will be exalted among the nations, I will be exalted in the earth! (Psalm 46:10 ESV)

The news will cut you to your core. Worldly issues that you can't control but stress over will break your heart. Ongoing issues in our world don't just happen overnight, so now is the time to take a breath and give it all to our Lord. Let go of the stress, the anger, the guilt, the frustration, the sadness and fear. Just let it go! It actually is that simple to do. Trusting in God's plan and praying to Him works more than we think. It helps us to slow down and relax. It helps us heal. Let Him help you! Let Him bring you relief! Let Him In! He is here with us, all of us.

Trust in the Lord with all your heart, and lean not on your own understanding. (Proverbs 3:5 ESV)

Personal Reflection . . .

_____

_____

_____

_____

_____

_____

_____

_____

_____

_____

_____

_____

Trust in the Lord with all thine heart; and lean not unto thine own understanding. (Proverbs 3:5 KJV)

❤With Hope Nothing Can Bring You Down❤

But in your hearts honor Christ the Lord as Holy, always being prepared to make a defense to anyone who asks you for a reason for the hope that is in you; yet do it with gentleness and respect.
(1 Peter 3:15 ESV)

Hope quite literally saves lives! It helps us to understand that our lives are worth living in the midst of chaos and uncertainty. Hope is a feeling of expectation and desire for a certain thing to happen. It's a wish, a goal, an aspiration and a feeling of trust. Does God not say to trust Him and to pray to Him? Does He not remind us to put our faith in Him? Situations we face on earth might seem hopeless, but when we put our faith in God, hope for a brighter tomorrow heals our sorrows. Start living with great expectation in your heart! Start hoping for something wonderful to happen!

~Hope in the Lord's Promises~

Personal Reflection . . .

_____

_____

_____

_____

_____

_____

_____

_____

Trust in the Lord with all thine heart; and lean not unto thine own understanding. (Proverbs 3:5 KJV)

❤ Service and Learning ❤

In all things I have shown you that by working hard in this way we must help the weak and remember the words of the Lord Jesus, how he himself said, "It is more blessed to give than to receive." (Acts 20:35 ESV)

The happiest I've ever seen my daughter was when she came home from our church's Youth Mission trip last summer. She was 16 years old and had traveled to West Virginia for five days to help repair homes. She'd made life-long friends, attended worship services, helped others and told me that her heart was touched in ways she could never describe. Upon her arrival back home, she was quiet and emotional. I thought she had had a rough week. Then, after speaking to her Youth leaders and friends, I found out that she smiled, laughed, danced, cared for others, cried for others, and in fact didn't want to leave. For any parent this is heartwarming news. She then opened up to me through tears that it was the best time she's ever had. She was out of her comfort zone and amongst people she didn't know very well. This is what mission trips are all about! Feeling the gratification of crying out of pure happiness. She learned, she grew from feeling the Holy Spirit, and she served others. And this is where she received pure happiness.

~Happiness is in the Holy Spirit~

Trust in the Lord with all thine heart; and lean not unto thine own understanding. (Proverbs 3:5 KJV)

Personal Reflection . . .

Trust in the Lord with all thine heart; and lean not unto thine own understanding. (Proverbs 3:5 KJV)

❤️*Knowledge*❤️

An intelligent heart acquires knowledge, and the ear of the wise seeks knowledge. (Proverbs 18:15 ESV)

The fear of the Lord is the beginning of knowledge; fools despise wisdom and instruction (Proverbs 1:7 ESV)

A wise man is full of strength, and a man of knowledge enhances his might. (Proverbs 24:5 ESV)

The heart of him who has understanding seeks knowledge, but the mouths of fools feed on folly. (Proverbs 15:14 ESV)

The meaning of Knowledge is containing facts, information and skills acquired by a person through experience or education. Facts, information and experience are all found in scripture. Reading Proverbs has opened my eyes to the importance of knowledge. When we seek to understand, it's important to read. When we seek knowledge on a topic, it's important to educate ourselves. Turning all of our time and attention to social media isn't going to give us answers, but the Bible will. Many of us can provide helpful ideas and concepts, but pure knowledge is attained by our own personal experience with scripture. The Bible has been passed down for centuries, generation after generation, for us to find knowledge, understanding and information to help guide and shape our lives.

Trust in the Lord with all thine heart; and lean not unto thine own understanding. (Proverbs 3:5 KJV)

Personal Reflection . . .

_____
_____
_____
_____
_____
_____
_____
_____
_____
_____
_____
_____
_____
_____
_____
_____
_____
_____
_____
_____
_____
_____
_____
_____
_____
_____
_____

Trust in the Lord with all thine heart; and lean not unto thine own understanding. (Proverbs 3:5 KJV)

♥Are You Worrying♥

Anxiety in a man's heart weighs him down, but a good word makes him glad. (Proverbs 12:25 ESV)

Worrying quite literally costs you everything! Your peace is worth more than your fears. Your joy and hope are worth more than your doubts. Do not let these be overcome by worrying about things that are out of your control. Tell God you trust Him in every situation. This is what He does! He works on our behalf. Just as we support our children and love them, take care of them and help them through every difficult situation, God also does this for His children. We are all His children. I know it can be very difficult to not worry about things, but it's not impossible!

Pray this day,
Trust in God this day,
Live in peace this day,
Be joyful this day.

Personal Reflection . . .

_____
_____
_____
_____
_____
_____
_____
_____
_____
_____

Trust in the Lord with all thine heart; and lean not unto thine own understanding. (Proverbs 3:5 KJV)

♥ *Love Means Everything* ♥

A sweet friendship refreshes the soul. (Proverbs 27:9 ESV)

What connections have you made in life with others? I love my family but I do not have sisters. I have two lovely sisters-in-law whom I love dearly. But my two very best friends I've known for over twenty years are like sisters to me. Life can be full of love. It is okay to open your heart and let people in. It is okay to love others and to let them love you. It is okay to pray for them, cherish them and defend them. Our God is wonderful in that He'll guide you to the right people to keep in your life. People who will support you, guide you, listen to you, help you and love you.

~Tell a very special friend in your life how much they mean to you~

Personal Reflection . . .

_____

_____

_____

_____

_____

_____

_____

_____

_____

_____

_____

Trust in the Lord with all thine heart; and lean not unto thine own understanding. (Proverbs 3:5 KJV)

❤*His Will Shall Be Done*❤

If anyone's will is to do God's will, he will know whether the teaching is from God or whether I am speaking on my own authority. The one who speaks on his own authority seeks his own glory; but the one who seeks the glory of him who sent him is true, and in him there is no falsehood (John 7:17-18 ESV)

Our faith leads us to Him.
Our faith allows us to hear from Him.
Our Faith is in Him.
His Will is for us, not against us.
His Word is strong, true and wise.
His way is the only way.
Speak with honor in His Holy name.
Speak of truth in His praise.
Speak of Love to Him and others.
I will trust in the Lord with all my heart.
I am not perfect but will follow His Word.
I am a child of God.

Personal Reflection . . .

_____
_____
_____
_____
_____
_____
_____
_____

Trust in the Lord with all thine heart; and lean not unto thine own understanding. (Proverbs 3:5 KJV)

❤*Onward to a Brighter Tomorrow*❤

Brothers, I do not consider that I have made it my own. But one thing I do: forgetting what lies behind and straining forward to what lies ahead, I press on toward the goal for the prize of the upward call of God in Christ Jesus. (Philippians 3:13-14 ESV)

What would a new beginning look like for you? Not everyone feels they need one, but if you've been stuck and are yearning for more in your life, how do you move forward? Change can be difficult and certainly scary, but it's important to remember that you'll never be moving forward by yourself. God has great things planned for each of us, but if we aren't willing to follow His call, then we'll never truly know what to do. I have found that hearing His call comes from being at your most vulnerable in life. When we pray from the depths of our hearts, we are truly awake to hearing His Word. It's amazing that He loves us and wants wonderful things for our future.

~Go to Him if you are in Need of Moving to a Brighter Tomorrow~

Personal Reflection . . .

_____

_____

_____

_____

_____

_____

_____

Trust in the Lord with all thine heart; and lean not unto thine own understanding. (Proverbs 3:5 KJV)

♥ Joy comes In the Morning from Knowing Your Worth ♥

For his anger endureth for a moment; in his favour is life: weeping may endure for a night, but joy cometh in the morning.
(Psalm 30:5 KJV)

There will be times in our lives when we are told we don't do enough, and that will question our purpose in life. Hard work comes in so many different shapes and forms! But unfortunately, if a pay check isn't connected to some of your hard work, it can be looked upon as not being work at all. Think about the work that Jesus performed. He traveled helping people, healing people, listening to and guiding others to the Word of God. And His name will forever be remembered. He didn't get a paycheck, and most of the time He was scoffed at. But what He did receive in return for His tremendous amount of work was gratitude. People yearned to be near Him, to feel His presence and love. His work was planned to guide those without faith and turn them into believers. His work was gentle but came with the biggest paycheck of all, His love and sacrifice for us. If you're struggling with sleeping at night over feeling worthy, pray and wake up with renewed positive attitude.

~I pray that you know that whatever your job is, you feel appreciated. Keep Jesus with you and continue to follow in His footsteps of hard work, love, discipline and gratitude~

Trust in the Lord with all thine heart; and lean not unto thine own understanding. (Proverbs 3:5 KJV)

Personal Reflection . . .

Trust in the Lord with all thine heart; and lean not unto thine own understanding. (Proverbs 3:5 KJV)

♥ *Seek Him Always* ♥

I sought the Lord and he answered me and delivered me from all my fears. (Psalm 34:4 ESV)

Seek Him through Prayer,
Seek Him through Love,
Seek Him through Meditation,
Seek Him through Helping Others,
Seek Him through Scripture,
Seek Him through Church,
Seek Him through your Struggles,
Seek Him through your Blessings,
Seek Him through Nature,
Seek Him through Family,
Seek Him Always.

Personal Reflection . . .

Trust in the Lord with all thine heart; and lean not unto thine own understanding. (Proverbs 3:5 KJV)

♥When Life Gets Busy, Have Some Fun♥

A joyful heart is good medicine, but a crushed spirit dries up the bones. (Proverbs 17:22 ESV)

Have you ever noticed that when you smile, laugh and dance that your mood dramatically improves? You can absolutely have fun and enjoy your life while working hard and being responsible. Life isn't all about being serious, paying bills and sleeping. Let us rejoice in the name of our Lord and praise His Holy name! Fill your days with joyful family moments, games, laughter and good company. If your life gets too busy and stressful, take a moment to plan something that fills your heart with excitement!

~ Every Soul Deserves to Rejoice~

Personal Reflection . . .

_____

_____

_____

_____

_____

_____

_____

_____

_____

_____

_____

_____

_____

Trust in the Lord with all thine heart; and lean not unto thine own understanding. (Proverbs 3:5 KJV)

♥*Saying Thank You Never Grows Old*♥

Give thanks in all circumstances; for this is the will of God in Christ Jesus for you. (1 Thessalonians 5:18 ESV)

Throughout my years of facing hardships, I've learned that saying thank you helps my heart recover. Without these struggles I would not have grown into the person I am today. How about you? What do you give thanks for? When scripture reminds us to "give thanks in all circumstances," this literally means to give thanks in every situation we face daily. Through the good and the bad, the happy and the sad, the big and the small, give thanks. Sometimes it may seem difficult to say thank you when we're sad and going through tough times, but these two words show character. Thank You God for teaching me, guiding me, loving me, sparing me, forgiving me and never leaving me when life gets tough.

~Thank You~

Personal Reflection . . .

_____
_____
_____
_____
_____
_____
_____
_____
_____
_____

Trust in the Lord with all thine heart; and lean not unto thine own understanding. (Proverbs 3:5 KJV)

♥ Just a Friendly Reminder ♥

While I live I praise the Lord: I will sing praises unto my God while I have any being. (Psalm 146:2 KJV)

Stop! Look! See! Life is amazing. Even through hardships we still have this awesome ability to live our lives full of joy and laughter. Let us celebrate the idea of living. So many people are fighting through illnesses and also the loss of loved ones they would give anything to have more time with. When we put ourselves in someone else's shoes, we can somewhat understand and experience what they're going through. These eye-opening times show us how to be grateful for what we have. Life is wonderful. Life is worth it. Life is irreplaceable.

~Give Thanks to our Lord above for this Wonderful Time we Have~

Personal Reflection . . .

_____

_____

_____

_____

_____

_____

_____

_____

_____

_____

_____

Trust in the Lord with all thine heart; and lean not unto thine own understanding. (Proverbs 3:5 KJV)

♥*Good Morning God*♥

I have set the Lord always before me. Because He is at my right hand, I will not be shaken. (Psalm 16:8)

Dear Heavenly Father,

I pray this morning that you use me as an instrument of your peace. Please direct my feet in the way you need them to go. Please place me in the path of those in need of kindness and those who need reminded of your good grace. I often fall short of your calling and will continue to keep my heart and mind open to hearing your words of guidance. Thank you for your everlasting love and mercy in my life and in the lives of those around me. I pray that everyone feeling lost, unforgiven or hopeless feel your eternal embrace wrapped around them. Help me to share your words of wisdom, truth, and encouragement with the world this day and every day. In Jesus name I pray, Amen.

Personal Reflection . . .

_____

_____

_____

_____

_____

_____

_____

_____

_____

_____

_____

Trust in the Lord with all thine heart; and lean not unto thine own understanding. (Proverbs 3:5 KJV)

♥ Home Is Where the Heart Is ♥

But as for me and my house, we will serve the Lord.
(Joshua 24:15 KJV)

God can be honored anywhere you desire. We openly pray at meals in our home, talk about the Bible, ask and answer questions and speak of His wonderful works. This specifically includes my four children. Allowing our Lord to be present brings great peace into our home. Home is an amazing place to be filled with love, communication, laughter and safety. It's a time of enjoyment, yet also a time of discipline and education on manners. If you grew up not having a positive family environment, it's never too late to have your own.

~Family, Faith, Fun~

Personal Reflection . . .

_____

_____

_____

_____

_____

_____

_____

_____

_____

_____

_____

_____

Trust in the Lord with all thine heart; and lean not unto thine own understanding. (Proverbs 3:5 KJV)

♥What's It Going to Take♥

But the righteous shall be glad; they shall exult before God; they shall be jubilant with joy. (Psalm 68:3 ESV)

Have you put taking care of yourself on the back burner? Living a Christian life means helping and caring for others as well as ourselves. We must continually fill our spiritual, mental and physical beings with God's Word and healthy options. We need rest, positive energy, exercise, scripture, and healthy food choices. Feeding our own souls helps us to feed others. When we take care of ourselves, our positive energy and spirit shines before those who need a fresh renewal of their faith. And when this happens, we indeed find the pure happiness we seek.

~Never Procrastinate in your own Happiness~

Personal Reflection . . .

_____
_____
_____
_____
_____
_____
_____
_____
_____
_____
_____
_____
_____

Trust in the Lord with all thine heart; and lean not unto thine own understanding. (Proverbs 3:5 KJV)

♥Take a Pause♥

Be still, and know that I am God. (Psalm 46:10 KJV)

Pause wherever you are and give thanks. Pause and take a deep breath! Pause and look up with a genuine heart. Just stop for a moment and relax in life. There is nothing too important right this second that should outweigh taking the time to just be still. Take a deep breath, inhaling our Lord's love and exhaling all your stress. That's right, just be still! Remember to whom you belong and bask in His loving grace. Life is too busy. Life is too complicated. Life is overwhelming. But life is always better with Him! Slowing down helps us to remember what is truly important.

~Trust Him, Go to Him, Rely on Him~

Personal Reflection . . .

_____

_____

_____

_____

_____

_____

_____

_____

_____

_____

_____

_____

Trust in the Lord with all thine heart; and lean not unto thine own understanding. (Proverbs 3:5 KJV)

❤️ *It's Never Too Late to Start Having Fun* ❤️

There is nothing better for a person than that he should eat and drink and find enjoyment in his toil. This also, I saw, is from the hand of God. (Ecclesiastes 2:24 ESV)

"Find enjoyment in his toil" …Toil means to work hard, exert oneself, strive, effort and labor. Any type of work plays a large role in our lives. And when work takes over, we tend to lose sight of enjoying precious moments in life. One example is just letting go and having fun! When we apply balance to our lives, work and fun can go hand in hand. Have you laughed recently? Have you played a game? Have you gone dancing, gone on a roller coaster or hung out with friends? There is always time for enjoyment and there is always time for laughter. Have fun today!

~Take a Deep Breath and just Enjoy your Life~

Personal Reflection . . .

_____

_____

_____

_____

_____

_____

_____

_____

_____

_____

_____

_____

_____

Trust in the Lord with all thine heart; and lean not unto thine own understanding. (Proverbs 3:5 KJV)

♥ Focus ♥

Set your mind on things that are above, not on things that are on earth. (Colossians 3:2 ESV)

Where is your focus today? Are you waking up stressed and uneasy with a mountain of things on your mind? Or are you joyful and ready to conquer the day? I woke up feeling a tad in between these two. What's weighing on my heart is the idea of there being children in our world who are homeless, abused, neglected and sad. Children are innocent and precious, so the idea of any of them crying due to abuse and loneliness absolutely breaks my heart. I have been praying on this issue for two days now. I decided to take my sadness and frustration to God and to raise these children up to Him in prayer! After feeling a bit of peace on this matter, I've decided to place my focus on my own children and the blessings in my life. It's important to pray for others while also enjoying what our Lord has placed before us.

~Focus your Heart, Mind and Spirit on things Above~

Personal Reflection . . .

Trust in the Lord with all thine heart; and lean not unto thine own understanding. (Proverbs 3:5 KJV)

♥ Balance ♥

To every thing there is a season, a time for every purpose under heaven:
A time to be born, and a time to die;
A time to plant, and a time to pluck what has been planted;
A time to kill, and a time to heal;
A time to break down, and a time build up;
A time to weep, and a time to laugh;
A time to mourn, and a time to dance;
A time to cast away stones, and a time to gather stones;
A time to embrace, and a time to refrain from embracing;
A time to gain, and a time to lose;
A time to keep, and a time to throw away;
A time to rend, and a time to sew;
A time to keep silence, and a time to speak;
A time to love, and a time to hate;
A time of war, and a time of peace.
(Ecclesiastes 3:1-8 KJV)

We will have to take the good with the bad in life. How do we deal with that? Balance. It is something to work on every single day. We must give thanks for the lessons we learn. We must love and be kind even in our darkest moments. We must be strong and have faith. We must cry and mourn all while acknowledging our blessings. Laughter through tears is an amazing feeling! Finding love after heartbreak cannot be matched! Accepting Jesus into our lives after years of doubt is beyond gratifying! I pray that you find the balance you are seeking.

Trust in the Lord with all thine heart; and lean not unto thine own understanding. (Proverbs 3:5 KJV)

Personal Reflection . . .

Trust in the Lord with all thine heart; and lean not unto thine own understanding. (Proverbs 3:5 KJV)

♥ My Secret is Simple, I Pray ♥

Dear Heavenly Father,

I pray this day for those who are grieving the loss of a loved one. I pray that they feel your everlasting love and embrace. Please watch over the broken-hearted and help them to find peace in these difficult times. I pray that family bonds are strong, never to be broken when they fall upon life's hardships. Please provide a wave of comfort for the broken-hearted. Life is full of tragic events, but when we remember that you are with us, it lightens these burdens we carry in our hearts. Thank you for your continued grace and thank you for being with us always. In Jesus name I pray, Amen.

Personal Reflection . . .

_____
_____
_____
_____
_____
_____
_____
_____
_____
_____
_____
_____
_____
_____
_____

Trust in the Lord with all thine heart; and lean not unto thine own understanding. (Proverbs 3:5 KJV)

❤Can You Imagine Not Having Him in Your Life❤

He will be our peace. (Micah 5:5 ESV)

These things I have spoken unto you, that in me ye might have peace. In the world ye shall have tribulation: but be of good cheer; I have overcome the world. (John 16:33 KJV)

If it seems impossible to obtain peace in this lifetime, rest assured that you can find peace in Him. You don't ever have to go through stress alone. If the news, parenting, your job, family life, illness, evil doers in our world, or loneliness are creating stress and uncertainty in your life, turn to God. You will always find peace in prayer and giving your troubles to Him. I do it almost every day! He is here to listen and to guide us through our journey on earth.

~Never will He Leave you Alone~

Personal Reflection . . .

Trust in the Lord with all thine heart; and lean not unto thine own understanding. (Proverbs 3:5 KJV)

♥His Promises Are Kept♥

If you need reminders of God's promises to help keep you going, here you go.

For all of the promises of God find their YES in him. That is why it is through Him that we utter Amen to God for His Glory.
(2 Corinthians 1:20 ESV)

And my God will supply every need of yours according to his riches in Glory in Christ Jesus. (Philippians 4:19 ESV)

For I know the plans I have for you, declares the Lord, plans for welfare and not for evil, to give you a future and a hope.
(Jeremiah 29:11 ESV)

Delight yourself in the Lord, and He will give you the desires of your heart. (Psalm 37:4 ESV)

Fear not, for I am with you; be not dismayed, for I am your God; I will strengthen you, I will help you, I will uphold you with my righteous right hand. (Isaiah 41:10 ESV)

Even if I walk through the valley of the shadow of death, I shall fear evil, for you are with me; your rod and your staff, they comfort me. (Psalm 23:4 ESV)

And this is the promise that He made to us - eternal life.
(1 John 2:25 ESV)

Trust in the Lord with all thine heart; and lean not unto thine own understanding. (Proverbs 3:5 KJV)

Personal Reflection . . .

_____
_____
_____
_____
_____
_____
_____
_____
_____
_____
_____
_____
_____
_____
_____
_____
_____
_____
_____
_____
_____
_____
_____
_____
_____
_____
_____
_____

Trust in the Lord with all thine heart; and lean not unto thine own understanding. (Proverbs 3:5 KJV)

♥ His Eyes Are on Us Always ♥

The eyes of the Lord are upon the righteous, and his ears are open unto their cry. (Psalm 34:15 KJV)

There will be periods of time where we fear He isn't with us. But His promises assure us that He will never leave. I love the idea of having Faith. It brings so much hope and contentment to our hearts. We should rejoice in His love for us! We should sing when we believe! Having God present in our lives is the greatest reassurance of things unknown and unseen. We can overcome fear, overcome hardships, and remain calm in a world full of stresses.

~For His eye is on the sparrow, and I know He watches me~

Personal Reflection . . .

_____

_____

_____

_____

_____

_____

_____

_____

_____

_____

_____

_____

_____

_____

Trust in the Lord with all thine heart; and lean not unto thine own understanding. (Proverbs 3:5 KJV)

♥There is Always Hope for You♥

More than that, we rejoice in our sufferings, knowing that suffering produces endurance, and endurance produces character, and character produces hope, and hope does not put us to shame, because God's love has been poured into our hearts through the Holy Spirit who has been given to us.
(Romans 5:3-5 ESV)

No matter your past or present failures, you can still be used as an instrument of His peace! His mercy and grace through Christ our Savior give us the strength and knowledge we need to turn our lives around. Do not let your missteps in life keep you from hoping for a better tomorrow. You are useful, you are important, you are needed and you are loved. When you seek our Lord, you will NEVER be turned away! You're a precious child of His everlasting goodness and grace. I pray this day that you truly understand and accept that Christ is for you, not against you.

~It's never too late to start over with our Lord~

Personal Reflection . . .

_____

_____

_____

_____

_____

_____

_____

_____

_____

_____

Trust in the Lord with all thine heart; and lean not unto thine own understanding. (Proverbs 3:5 KJV)

♥Get Excited♥

The heart of man plans his way, but the Lord establishes his steps. (Proverbs 16:9 ESV)

Who's excited to see what God has planned for them? So many of us grow up not knowing what we want to do in life. Which career to start, which college to attend, which church to join, to start a family or not start a family, and so on. I think we all at one time or another ask "what should I do?" Answers don't come overnight, but when we open our hearts in genuine prayer to God, He will guide us. It's exciting to know that good things are still to come for us all! It's amazing to know that He wants us to be joyful, He wants us to live well, and He wants us to trust in His plan for our lives.

~Be Excited for Everything Today~

Personal Reflection . . .

Trust in the Lord with all thine heart; and lean not unto thine own understanding. (Proverbs 3:5 KJV)

♥ Look unto Him ♥

For I am sure that neither death nor life, nor angels nor rulers, nor things present nor things to come, nor powers, nor height nor depth, nor anything else in all creation, will be able to separate us from the love of God in Christ Jesus our Lord. (Romans 8:38-39 ESV)

When we love, we forgive. We listen, we truly hear. When we seek our Lord with a righteous heart, He is with us always. Nothing can separate us from His everlasting love. In all situations, pray. In all situations, give thanks! In all situations, look up. Never give up, never let go, and never fail to turn to Him for guidance.

~Look unto Him in Every Way~

Personal Reflection . . .

_____

_____

_____

_____

_____

_____

_____

_____

_____

_____

_____

_____

Trust in the Lord with all thine heart; and lean not unto thine own understanding. (Proverbs 3:5 KJV)

❤ There Are No Words ❤

But in your hearts honor Christ the Lord as holy, always being prepared to make a defense to anyone who asks you for a reason for the hope that is in you; yet do it with gentleness and respect.
(1 Peter 3:15 ESV)

To explain to others what Jesus means to me is difficult to express in words. The spiritual feelings I have are unmeasurable! I have been tried and tested, but my instinctive reactions toward Christ are strong, overwhelming, and emotional. I've learned through my hardships, others hardships, and through what goes on in the world that I will fight for His namesake more than I ever thought I would. My love for Him is eternal. My fight for Him is everlasting. My representation of Him is gentle.

Personal Reflection . . .

Trust in the Lord with all thine heart; and lean not unto thine own understanding. (Proverbs 3:5 KJV)

♥*Glory be to God*♥

Arise, shine, for your light has come, and the glory of the Lord has risen upon you. (Isaiah 60:1 ESV)

God is everywhere we are. He is in the air we breathe, the sun that shines down on our skin, and the birds singing His beautiful song. Our faith won't just move mountains, it will move our souls and others into His glorious light. Let His presence embrace you in your daily tasks. Let Him guide you into doing His work through your words and actions. Let Him in.

~Glory be to God in the highest, and let your hearts be filled with peace~

Personal Reflection . . .

_____

_____

_____

_____

_____

_____

_____

_____

_____

_____

_____

_____

_____

_____

Trust in the Lord with all thine heart; and lean not unto thine own understanding. (Proverbs 3:5 KJV)

♥ Pray for Your Children ♥

But the helper, the Holy Spirit, whom the Father will send in my name, He will teach you all things and bring to your remembrance all that I have said to you. (John 14:26 ESV)

Right vs. wrong is something we assume our children know. But in a world filled with distractions, temptations and violence, we must remember to speak to them daily as well as praying for them. It's never too early or too late to introduce them to Jesus. For Jesus said, "Let the children come to me, and do not hinder them, for to such belongs the kingdom of God" (Luke 18:16). Our children deserve love, respect, and our continued knowledge on living a fulfilling life of righteousness. Pray for them daily, speak to them on the truth and wisdom of scripture, and tell them they are loved beyond measure.

~ God Bless our Children~

Personal Reflection . . .

_____

_____

_____

_____

_____

_____

_____

_____

_____

_____

_____

Trust in the Lord with all thine heart; and lean not unto thine own
understanding. (Proverbs 3:5 KJV)

❤ How Are We Inspiring Others ❤

And let us consider how to stir up one another to love and good works, not neglecting to meet together, as is the habit of some, but encouraging one another, and all the more as you see the day drawing near. (Hebrews 10:24-25 ESV)

Whether we see it or not, our positive attitudes are contagious. I definitely remember when people were kind to me as I was struggling. Reaching out, listening, giving advice and being a helping hand go much further than we think. Don't ever go through life thinking it's not your place to help someone. The least we could all do is to pray for those who are facing hardships.

~Prayers are love, Caring is love, Being positive is love~

Personal Reflection . . .

_____
_____
_____
_____
_____
_____
_____
_____
_____
_____
_____
_____
_____
_____

Trust in the Lord with all thine heart; and lean not unto thine own understanding. (Proverbs 3:5 KJV)

❤What Does the Cross Mean to You❤

I have been crucified with Christ. It is no longer I who live, but Christ who lives in me. And the life I now live in the flesh I live by faith in the Son of God, who loved me and gave himself for me. (Galatians 2:20 ESV)

Being a true Christian isn't comfortable. It means putting yourself out in the world in the name of Christ. It's about taking up your cross and following Jesus. If we continued to stay in our comfortable bubbles, we would not grow. We would not learn, or educate or inspire others who are in need of direction. If we conform to others ideals and beliefs because they are simply offended, then we have let down the one who sacrificed everything to give us life. To stand up for Him is love. It's commitment, it's respect and it's something He would do all over again for us.

~It Means Everything~

Personal Reflection . . .

_____

_____

_____

_____

_____

_____

_____

_____

_____

_____

Trust in the Lord with all thine heart; and lean not unto thine own understanding. (Proverbs 3:5 KJV)

❤ May the Lord Bless you and Keep You Forever ❤

Abide in me, and I in you. As the branch cannot bear fruit of itself, except it abide in the vine; no more can ye, except ye abide in me. (John 15:4 KJV)

Dear Heavenly Father,

I pray this day that those who are weary and burdened turn to you. I pray they find comfort in abiding in your love, grace, and comfort. May everyone pray to you in their struggles and times of happiness. For you are the one true God who fills our hearts with peace. You lift us when we fall and give us the courage to speak of your Holy name. Please continue to bless and guide those who are in search of your presence. Help us all to be mindful of showing kindness and love in the name of Christ Jesus. Amen

Personal Reflection . . .

Trust in the Lord with all thine heart; and lean not unto thine own understanding. (Proverbs 3:5 KJV)

♥Your Faith can Move Mountains but your Doubt can Create Them♥

But let him ask in faith, with no doubting, for the one who doubts is like a wave of the sea that is driven and tossed by the wind. (James 1:6 ESV)

Who creates problems that don't exist? I definitely do. Overthinking and doubting cannot just ruin your mood, it can ruin your relationships. Sometimes it's difficult to get out of your own head. I truly believe that this is when we must turn to scripture for guidance. If we can singlehandedly ruin relationships with our insecurities, we must remember that our relationship with God can also be severed. Having faith is going to keep our relationship strong! And when we have faith, we have confidence. When we have confidence, we lack doubt. So, conquer your doubts by increasing your faith. It's something we must practice every day.

Personal Reflection . . .

_____

_____

_____

_____

_____

_____

_____

_____

_____

_____

Trust in the Lord with all thine heart; and lean not unto thine own understanding. (Proverbs 3:5 KJV)

❤ Think Before You React ❤

But the fruit of the spirit is love, joy, peace, longsuffering, gentleness, goodness, faith, meekness, temperance: against such there is no law. (Galatians 5:22-23 KJV)

Let me just say that it's no secret that being kind to rude people is hard! I've thought about being rude back sometimes, but when I've chosen kindness, I've walked away feeling completely proud of myself. We often don't take those few seconds to think before reacting. When we stop, take a breath, and ask God to be with us, we remember that He's watching. This provides positive energy that feeds our souls. He doesn't want people to walk all over us or be rude to us, but He also doesn't want us to do the same. We have absolutely no idea how our kindness actually affects people behind the scenes. It's always worth doing the right thing in a negative situation! Your character means everything.

~Don't treat people as bad as they are, treat people as good as you are~

Personal Reflection . . .

_____

_____

_____

_____

_____

_____

_____

_____

Trust in the Lord with all thine heart; and lean not unto thine own understanding. (Proverbs 3:5 KJV)

♥The Lord is My Shepherd♥

The Lord is my Shepherd; I shall not want. He maketh me to lie down in green pastures; He leadeth me beside the still waters. He restoreth my soul; He leadeth me in the paths of righteousness for His name's sake. (Psalm 23:1-3 KJV)

"He restoreth my soul"! I am overwhelmed with great comfort when I read this passage. The Bible has given beautiful reminders of His grace, love and compassion for us. "I shall not want" tells us that everything we have in Christ is all we need. Worldly possessions will fade away, but His love and presence are everlasting. It's important to turn to Him in every way! If you've ever had questions, concerns or doubts, now is the time to face them. He is open and willing to accept you now and forever.

~I Shall Not Want~

Personal Reflection . . .

_____
_____
_____
_____
_____
_____
_____
_____
_____
_____
_____
_____

Trust in the Lord with all thine heart; and lean not unto thine own understanding. (Proverbs 3:5 KJV)

♥ *Love Every Minute with Him* ♥

Blessed be the God and Father of our Lord Jesus Christ, the Father of mercies and God of all comfort, who comforts us in all our affliction, so that we may be able to comfort those who are in any affliction, with the comfort with which we ourselves are comforted by God. (2 Corinthians 1:3-4 ESV)

Comfort, Love, Peace and Acceptance are qualities that Jesus provides in our times of need. Have you been through lonely times where you turned to Christ in prayer for comfort? I sure have. And even now when I'm struggling internally, I instinctively turn to Him for comfort. I actually look forward to it. He is the greatest gift we could have ever received. And He's not just for me or for you, He's for everyone. We are His beloved children who He has promised never to leave alone.

~Go to Him, Talk to Him, Draw Near to Him~

Personal Reflection . . .

_____
_____
_____
_____
_____
_____
_____
_____
_____
_____
_____

Trust in the Lord with all thine heart; and lean not unto thine own understanding. (Proverbs 3:5 KJV)

♥ *Nice vs. Kind* ♥

Let us not become weary in doing good. (Galatians 6:9 ESV)

There's a big difference between being nice to someone and being kind to someone. Both are important but different from one another. Nice means being pleasant or agreeable. Kindness means character, nature and quality. I can be nice to someone by saying "I like your outfit" or "hi, how are you today?" Then I can be kind by listening to someone's cries when they're struggling. I can send cards with encouraging words or watch someone's child when they have a family emergency. Kindness is everlasting and it's something others will never forget. It's going out of our way to truly help someone from the bottom of our hearts. It's volunteering, donating money, helping someone cross the street, making someone laugh and smile, offering help, or not judging others but listening to them. Kindness is something you feel while helping others.

~If you want to lift yourself up, reach out and help someone else~

Personal Reflection . . .

_____
_____
_____
_____
_____
_____
_____
_____
_____

Trust in the Lord with all thine heart; and lean not unto thine own
understanding. (Proverbs 3:5 KJV)

♥You Are So Loved♥

Strength and dignity are her clothing, and she laughs at the time to come. She opens her mouth with wisdom, and the teaching of kindness is on her tongue. (Proverbs 31:25-26 ESV)

Mothers out there, I love you, God loves you and your children love you. Even children who seem to take you for granted at times still love you. Love is inevitable, and everyone, regardless of their relationship, loves their mother. Children out there, take this day to pray for your mother. Tell her you love her and appreciate all of the hard work she has done for you.

~God Bless All the Mothers~

Personal Reflection . . .

Trust in the Lord with all thine heart; and lean not unto thine own understanding. (Proverbs 3:5 KJV)

Author's Bio

My name is Jennifer Taylor. As a young girl, I knew God was present in my life. I remember praying for world peace, although I never really understood what that meant, and also acknowledging that there was a constant presence around me. I became a mother at the age of 21 to my daughter, Audrey. Even then, I knew she as a gift from God. At the age of 23, after the birth of my second child, Danny, I was very busy and everyday life became a constant struggle. Yet, through it all, I still continued to pray.

Fast forward to age 36. I was now the mother of two more boys, Nathan and JT (James), and found myself remarried to a wonderful man. My children and I became members of an amazingly supportive church. This was where I heard that powerful call from the Holy Spirit telling me to start writing. I had been struggling with the idea of wanting to help people, but with four children and a tight budget, helping others seemed more like a dream than a reality. Little did I know that writing would be my way of helping others. The call was a soft yet precise voice, very distinct and exact in its message. Full of questions and doubt, I initially ignored my calling. The next month I heard it again, but this time it was in the form of a command. I followed its instruction and immediately began writing *Daily Devotions with Jen*.

I had fears of being ridiculed, blasphemed and hated for writing about God's Word. I then realized that, when you are called to act on his behalf, you listen, follow and be brave. God knew I was capable more than I knew myself. I knew that, given his instruction, and blessed with courage, I could go outside my comfort zone and proceed to this calling.

October 30, 2015, marks the first day of my writing journey. Through scripture I have been able to help others reaffirm their faith and hope in God's love for them. This journey has helped me understand that we are all called to ministry in one way or another. It is through us that God's word is taught, heard, obeyed and trusted.

Also I heard the voice of the Lord, saying, whom shall I send, and who will go for us? Then said I, Here am I; send me. (Isaiah 6:8 KJV)

43581935R00095

Made in the USA
San Bernardino, CA
15 July 2019